Poems

as

Friends

Fiona Bennett
& Michael Shaeffer

Poems
as
Friends

The Poetry Exchange
10th Anniversary
Anthology

QUERCUS

First published in Great Britain in 2024 by

QUERCUS

Quercus Editions Ltd
Carmelite House
50 Victoria Embankment
London EC4Y 0DZ

An Hachette UK company

See page 169 for Permissions Credits.

A CIP catalogue record for this book is available from the British Library.

HB ISBN 978 1 52943 245 9
Ebook ISBN 978 1 52943 246 6

10 9 8 7 6 5 4 3 2 1

Designed and typeset by EM&EN
Printed and bound in Great Britain by Clays Ltd, Elcograf S.p.A.

MIX
Paper | Supporting
responsible forestry
FSC
www.fsc.org   FSC® C104740

Papers used by Quercus Editions Ltd are from well-managed forests
and other responsible sources.

To our friends

Someone writing a poem believes . . . that an 'I' can become a 'we' . . . that a partly common language exists to which strangers can bring their own heartbeat, memories, images.

– Adrienne Rich, *What Is Found There*

Contents

The Friend that Helps Me Wrestle with the Difficult Things

The Friend That Names My Experience

xi

Introduction

This anthology is a celebration of the power of poetry in people's lives. It gathers together a selection of material drawn from ten years of The Poetry Exchange, an award-winning project and podcast that hosts conversations with readers about the poem that's been a friend to them. In the pages that follow you will find sixty poems, each person's chosen poem accompanied by their story of connection to it. Great poets of the past and present are brought together here in a rich and diverse gathering. The selection of poems has been made by readers from all walks of life and is drawn from our archive of over three hundred nominations from across the world.

Being introduced to poems by the readers for whom they have meant so much has been a moving, uplifting and nourishing experience. Over the years a wonderful community has gathered around the work, and together we have encountered poems we did not know before as well as being introduced anew to those we did. The invitation for people to talk about poems in this way led to such extraordinary and eloquent insights that we wanted to find a way to share these uniquely intimate conversations more widely. We began the podcast in 2016 and discovered poems as friends resonating with listeners across the world, with thousands tuning in every month. We are delighted that with this anthology we can extend our celebration of the companionship of poetry into book form. Michael Shaeffer, my long-time leading collaborator and co-host, is my co-author, and together we have had a fascinating experience delving into The Poetry Exchange archive to create this book.

The idea of poems as friends began when I recognized the powerful conversations I have with poems that have been there for me at key moments in my life, and became curious about whether this idea of a poem acting as a companion was true for others. Friendship is where we meet ourselves in commonality and diversity, where we celebrate shared loves and grapple with difference. Poems, like friends, can create a space for intimacy, mark occasions, events and ideas, and like true friends they can also have a presence beyond the here and now. As Michael and I explored the archive, reviewing audio files, reading through letters from readers and curating the material, different themes associated with friendship emerged. We have divided the book into five sections that reflect these themes. You will find here poems that sit with you in the dark and poems that bring the light, poems of celebration, elegy and comfort. There are also poems that might, like a good friend, challenge you to confront the thought that unsettles you or the truth you've felt in your bones but not yet found the words for.

We each meet a poem in our own way. The accompanying passages here focus on the personal connection our guests make with the poem, rather than any kind of definitive account of it, or exposition of the poet's work. The accounts celebrate the personal stories of readers, many of whom are writers too, and reveal how a poem acts as a carrier-wave of lived experience.

The passages have in the main been drawn from the audio recordings of the conversations held over the last ten years, and some were developed from letters we received. As we began this process, we were moved and lit up again by stories we had heard initially in voice form, now finding their register on the page. Each of these passages acts as a kind of short lyric essay inviting you towards the poem, or offering a coda of reflection to follow it. To that end we invite you to explore as you will, to read either the poem or the passage first, allowing your own resonances to flow in and out of the threads of connection offered.

I am grateful to the many wonderful people who have been the best of friends to this project and this book. They are the careful listeners, the editors, conversation hosts, producers, administrators and ambassadors who have kept the labour of love pumped with joy and wonder, and who have archived diligently and brought this book into the world.

They are listed at the end of the book, alongside the poets whose work is featured and the contributors who have trusted us with their stories.

So as you head into this gathering of poems as friends, we hope you'll enjoy reacquainting yourself with old companions, meeting some new ones, and extending the conversation about the way poetry plays a part in our lives.

Fiona Bennett, May 2023

The Friend that Offers Connection and Solidarity

Remember *by* Joy Harjo

The poem that's been a friend to Rachel Eliza Griffiths

I love Joy Harjo. She's an extraordinary woman and presence and music in the world.

A close friend sent me this poem as a gift when I was intensely grieving my mother's death. I've carried it on airplanes, across state lines, different countries, continents. It became a kind of incantation, I would even dare say prayer.

The poem is like a compass to me. I have it printed on little pieces of paper that I carry with me in my bag or my wallet. I'll be out somewhere, or on a journey, and if things are beyond my control, I'll just take it out and hold it. This gentle command: 'Remember.'

It invites meditation, daring you to recall those things that make you who you are. So it can travel with you literally, but it also travels through the arteries of your own autobiography, your own little tributaries of where you've been stuck or drowned or sailing through. Reading the poem, wherever I am, is a balm against loneliness or grief.

Sometimes we get isolated in our own experiences, and we feel alone. The poem asks you to step back, think of the whole constellation, and to remember all of us are here. What can we do for each other? What can we be toward one another? I often think at the end of each day: what have I done today? What have I offered? Was there something I gave with no expectation to get anything back? Service and citizenship are very important to me, because I know what it feels like to be looked at as someone who doesn't matter, someone who's at the margin. I can't control that, but I can control what I choose to give my memory to.

This poem is a friend of my mind, and it is a friend of my heart.

Remember

Remember the sky that you were born under,
know each of the star's stories.
Remember the moon, know who she is.
Remember the sun's birth at dawn, that is the
strongest point of time. Remember sundown
and the giving away to night.
Remember your birth, how your mother struggled
to give you form and breath. You are evidence of
her life, and her mother's, and hers.
Remember your father. He is your life, also.
Remember the earth whose skin you are:
red earth, black earth, yellow earth, white earth
brown earth, we are earth.
Remember the plants, trees, animal life who all have their
tribes, their families, their histories, too. Talk to them,
listen to them. They are alive poems.
Remember the wind. Remember her voice. She knows the
origin of this universe.
Remember you are all people and all people
are you.
Remember you are this universe and this
universe is you.
Remember all is in motion, is growing, is you.
Remember language comes from this.
Remember the dance language is, that life is.
Remember.

Joy Harjo

Song of Myself, V *by* Walt Whitman

The poem that's been a friend to Andrea Holland

An old friend of mine sent me a postcard and on the back all they had written was, 'Loafe with me on the grass, loose the stop from your throat, / not words, not music or rhyme I want, not custom or lecture, not even the best'. To get just that on the back of a postcard felt like a statement of deep human connection; it meant so much to me. I still have it up by my desk, twenty-seven years later.

I get really excited by the idea of this man celebrating the body in 1855 when the culture was all about covering up. I love the earnest and passionate language, the way that it marries together complicated things about the body and the self.

Again and again, I am drawn to this voice that asks us to recognize the complexities of a Self. 'I believe in you my soul, the other I am' – that duality between us as bodies, and us as spiritual beings. It's a true and genuine voice, speaking out over time, offering a sense of connection to lived experience.

I find the language comforting – the cadence, the rhythm, the way the words dance along the line. It becomes like a prayer or a song – it's enchanting, mesmerizing and musical.

'All the men ever born are also my brothers, and the women my sisters and lovers, and that a kelson of the creation is love'. It's such a simple statement about love and yet it feels so powerful and political and true.

It's about real kindness and understanding. Those moments of being honest with each other, being vulnerable, spending time feeling the sun on your face, noticing the pile of stones, and reaching to somebody's 'bare-stript heart'.

Song of Myself, V

I believe in you my soul, the other I am must not abase itself
    to you,
And you must not be abased to the other.

Loafe with me on the grass, loose the stop from your throat,
Not words, not music or rhyme I want, not custom or lecture,
    not even the best,
Only the lull I like, the hum of your valvèd voice.

I mind how once we lay such a transparent summer morning,
How you settled your head athwart my hips and gently turn'd
    over upon me,
And parted the shirt from my bosom-bone, and plunged your
    tongue to my bare-stript heart,
And reach'd till you felt my beard, and reach'd till you held
    my feet.

Swiftly arose and spread around me the peace and knowledge
    that pass all the argument of the earth,
And I know that the hand of God is the promise of my own,
And I know that the spirit of God is the brother of my own,
And that all the men ever born are also my brothers, and the
    women my sisters and lovers,
And that a kelson of the creation is love,
And limitless are leaves stiff or drooping in the fields,
And brown ants in the little wells beneath them,
And mossy scabs of the worm fence, heap'd stones, elder,
    mullein and poke-weed.

Walt Whitman

A Short Story of Falling *by* Alice Oswald

The poem that's been a friend to Charlie Beaumont

I first read this poem the minute it was published – I buy every collection she writes as soon as it comes out.

This poem has the life-giving force of nature running through it. It's got physicality and spirituality. You feel like you can touch what she's talking about. There's an immediate understanding on the first read and then you keep discovering more. There is so much in it. It feels like the water flows and the poem flows. It has a circular element to it that is like the never-ending cycle of rain.

I try and get stuck into poetry every day. You can get so much just by taking in one or two poems. I always carry a collection around in my bag, that I can just dip into. I love walking through the woods and reading poetry aloud, very loudly in fact. I have once or twice fallen over! I can feel quite stuck with a poem until I read it out loud, when suddenly it unfolds a bit and you realize where the breath of the poem is.

I used to work as a probation officer and did a lot of writing with prisoners and offenders. Poetry was a way of conducting a relationship, of having a conversation. They would write a poem and then I could respond with one. It created a levelling opportunity and opened a different channel of communication.

I'm attracted to poetry that reflects my own values. I feel like Oswald has got life's priorities right – relationships and the importance of looking after nature. I love the couplet, 'then I might know like water how to balance / the weight of hope, against the light of patience'.

A Short Story of Falling

It is the story of the falling rain
to turn into a leaf and fall again

it is the secret of a summer shower
to steal the light and hide it in a flower

and every flower a tiny tributary
that from the ground flows green and momentary

is one of water's wishes and this tale
hangs in a seed-head smaller than my thumbnail

if only I a passerby could pass
as clear as water through a plume of grass

to find the sunlight hidden at the tip
turning to seed a kind of lifting rain drip

then I might know like water how to balance
the weight of hope against the light of patience

water which is so raw so earthy-strong
and lurks in cast-iron tanks and leaks along

drawn under gravity towards my tongue
to cool and fill the pipe-work of this song

which is the story of the falling rain
that rises to the light and falls again

Alice Oswald

There was a Boy *by* William Wordsworth

The poem that's been a friend to Joe Hedinger

This poem has haunted me since I first read it. Where you are as the reader shifts as the poem progresses. It's about a boy having a moment of communion with the owls, but the bit that really strikes you is when he makes the call, and the owls don't call back. The whole world is suddenly inside him in the silence.

Like a lot of people, I became and still am very concerned about the environmental crisis. We want so desperately in a situation like this to connect with nature. In the poem, the deeper communion only happens when he stops trying – when he simply exists. It's calm and beautiful, but there's also a strangeness. To have a poem that taps into these moments of slight uncanniness, moments when you suddenly realize that maybe we haven't worked it all out yet, is wonderful. The feeling that there's something going on just off to the side of our vision, and maybe sitting with that strangeness and ambiguity is a good place to start.

Then there is this shift; there's a gap, he tells you the boy is dead, and suddenly we realize the narrator is in the poem and we're standing next to him by the boy's grave. We aren't outside the poem; we were in it all along. Just like ecology; it isn't 'over there', we are it. The writing is doing these complex, philosophical, and quite creepy judo flips.

This poem puts me in a state of anxiety, but I make friends with that anxiety. It's not giving me a hug; it's opening a door, jolting me. It's probably one of the first experiences where I felt like a poem was reading me as much as I was reading it.

There was a Boy

There was a Boy; ye knew him well, ye cliffs
And islands of Winander! many a time,
At evening, when the earliest stars began
To move along the edges of the hills,
Rising or setting, would he stand alone,
Beneath the trees, or by the glimmering lake;
And there, with fingers interwoven, both hands
Pressed closely palm to palm and to his mouth
Uplifted, he, as through an instrument,
Blew mimic hootings to the silent owls
That they might answer him.—And they would shout
Across the watery vale, and shout again,
Responsive to his call,—with quivering peals,
And long halloos, and screams, and echoes loud
Redoubled and redoubled; concourse wild
Of jocund din! And, when there came a pause
Of silence such as baffled his best skill:
Then, sometimes, in that silence, while he hung
Listening, a gentle shock of mild surprise
Has carried far into his heart the voice
Of mountain-torrents; or the visible scene
Would enter unawares into his mind
With all its solemn imagery, its rocks,
Its woods, and that uncertain heaven received
Into the bosom of the steady lake.

This boy was taken from his mates, and died
In childhood, ere he was full twelve years old.
Pre-eminent in beauty is the vale
Where he was born and bred: the churchyard hangs
Upon a slope above the village-school;

And through that churchyard when my way has led
On summer-evenings, I believe that there
A long half-hour together I have stood
Mute—looking at the grave in which he lies!

William Wordsworth

Spring and Fall *by* Gerard Manley Hopkins

The poem that's been a friend to
Anthony Vahni Capildeo

I read this poem as a child growing up in Trinidad. The leaves and flowers from the local trees there really do fall, so my first meeting with the poem made me do something that Hopkins would have appreciated – it made me look in praise at the particularity of nature surrounding me. I think for Hopkins there was something plantlike or treelike about human beings.

I used to climb the bookshelves in the house like a climbing frame. I found a collection of personal essays by Jean Kerr, called *Penny Candy*. She describes a scene where the family is gathered, and one of her sons reads 'Spring and Fall' and she begins to weep. So I encountered this poem as something that a child could read to a parent and make the parent reconnect with some truth of experience. That spring of immediate feeling, both sorrowful and joyful at once.

It's a bit like a dance. A poem that holds hands with you going round and round. It's the sense of that recurrence, and the endless springing of life. Whatever you might be feeling at an emotional level, there is a deeper movement of living in which you are involved, a recurrent pattern of refreshment. When Hopkins is talking about inscape, he doesn't just mean looking at the leaf and drawing it in a diagrammatic way. To apprehend inscape, there's that process of the pencil or pen repeatedly leaving the page, going back; of looking and looking again at the cloud or the leaf or the running water. That was how he apprehended the world; that's the vitality in which we share.

It's a friend to me as a writer, because I first read it early enough to be inoculated with a fearlessness about loving music and language, and to trust what happens when language begins to collapse and wants to go beyond itself.

Spring and Fall

to a young child

Márgarét, áre you gríeving
Over Goldengrove unleaving?
Leáves like the things of man, you
With your fresh thoughts care for, can you?
Ah! ás the heart grows older
It will come to such sights colder
By and by, nor spare a sigh
Though worlds of wanwood leafmeal lie;
And yet you wíll weep and know why.
Now no matter, child, the name:
Sórrow's spríngs áre the same.
Nor mouth had, no nor mind, expressed
What heart heard of, ghost guessed:
It ís the blight man was born for,
It is Margaret you mourn for.

Gerard Manley Hopkins

Ars Poetica #100: I Believe *by* Elizabeth Alexander

The poem that's been a friend to John Prebble

I love poetry. I love reading it, and I particularly love hearing it and reciting it. I first heard this in a barn at a literature festival, during a performance where three actors were weaving poems together. I vividly remember the moment of this particular poem, how it resonated with my feelings about poetry and the things that matter most to me.

I'm so pleased that my first encounter with this poem was hearing it read aloud, poetry being 'the human voice'. That claim, for me, has so many personal resonances. I was a chorister at Canterbury Cathedral – it was a hugely collaborative life and endeavour. I don't sing very much now, but those moments when you get to sing with a group, that electricity, just listening to each other, is still one of the most powerful things I have experienced. I often think about why hearing poetry matters so much to me, and it is that one voice connecting that literally resonates inside me.

This poem introduces you to poetry from lots of different angles, making claims of the heart and the head. I don't know where the poet is positioned in relation to these claims, but I like that it tests which bit I believe in most. I enjoy that invitation to think about things differently, to be creative, to trust how you feel about something and to be open about that. It's a poem about the permission to say: I Believe.

I'm interested in how personal this can be, despite the grandness of the themes. The way it resolves towards the end: 'Poetry is the human voice, and are we not of interest to each other?' I know I'll come back to this poem and it will keep reminding me of my essential beliefs. It gives me an anchor.

Ars Poetica #100: I Believe

Poetry, I tell my students,
is idiosyncratic. Poetry

is where we are ourselves
(though Sterling Brown said

"Every 'I' is a dramatic 'I'"),
digging in the clam flats

for the shell that snaps,
emptying the proverbial pocketbook.

Poetry is what you find
in the dirt in the corner,

overhear on the bus, God
in the details, the only way

to get from here to there.
Poetry (and now my voice is rising)

is not all love, love, love,
and I'm sorry the dog died.

Poetry (here I hear myself loudest)
is the human voice,

and are we not of interest to each other?

Elizabeth Alexander

Having a Coke with You *by* Frank O'Hara

The poem that's been a friend to Rishi Dastidar

Frank O'Hara is the perfect mid-century flâneur. An urban wanderer driven by the sensibility of being alive in the city. I'm very much a city person myself, wandering around observing people, imagining stories, and then suddenly I discover this notion of 'being a flâneur' that I can use to actually describe what it is that I do!

You can hear the jazz in this poem, that New York rhythm, that speed of urban living. There is such skill in the way he controls tone and pace. It's a touchstone for me as a writer.

I came to poetry quite late, with a stereotypical idea of English poetry as having to be in a very controlled rhythmic and metrical form, so O'Hara opened things right up for me. Suddenly, here was poetry that felt modern, poetry for the world, as it is lived now.

O'Hara celebrates the moment of love, but this is not a simple 'I'm in love with you' poem. The seduction here carries more reflection than that. There's adoration, but he also explores the ways in which we try to impress someone. He's mocking the persona of the shy unrequited lover, and the ending is almost an instruction to put themselves out there, risk love, say it, and who knows what might happen? It's a wonderful, effortless celebration of spontaneity.

There is a myth that as poets we must be strained and serious, plumbing our depths to get the good stuff out. O'Hara gives you permission for joy and for dwelling on the surfaces of things. You can see there is a very serious and quite moral guide there as well, but the morality is not at the expense of joy. Why would you not try and hymn those times when you actually felt alive, above and outside of yourself, those moments of transcendence?

Having a Coke with You

is even more fun than going to San Sebastian, Irún,
        Hendaye, Biarritz, Bayonne
or being sick to my stomach on the Travesera de
        Gracia in Barcelona
partly because in your orange shirt you look like a
        better happier St. Sebastian
partly because of my love for you, partly because
        of your love for yoghurt
partly because of the fluorescent orange tulips
        around the birches
partly because of the secrecy our smiles take on
        before people and statuary
it is hard to believe when I'm with you that there
        can be anything as still
as solemn as unpleasantly definitive as statuary
        when right in front of it
in the warm New York 4 o'clock light we are
        drifting back and forth
between each other like a tree breathing through its
        spectacles

and the portrait show seems to have no faces in it
        at all, just paint
you suddenly wonder why in the world anyone
        ever did them
                        I look
at you and I would rather look at you than all the
        portraits in the world
except possibly for the *Polish Rider* occasionally
        and anyway it's in the Frick
which thank heavens you haven't gone to yet so we
        can go together for the first time

and the fact that you move so beautifully more or
        less takes care of Futurism
just as at home I never think of the *Nude
        Descending a Staircase* or
at a rehearsal a single drawing of Leonardo or
        Michelangelo that used to wow me
and what good does all the research of the
        Impressionists do them
when they never got the right person to stand near
        the tree when the sun sank
or for that matter Marino Marini when he didn't
        pick the rider as carefully
as the horse
                it seems they were all cheated of some
        marvelous experience
which is not going to go wasted on me which is
        why I'm telling you about it

                                        Frank O'Hara

Love (III) *by* George Herbert

The poem that's been a friend to Andrew Scott

I think it's just so beautiful, 'Love bade me welcome.' It's the very first thing, there was no struggle to make that invitation, he simply says welcome, and I think that's why this poem has been a friend to me. Many of us feel undeserving of love. If you don't feel like you're worthy of love, you can't access the very thing that you really need and that's terribly sad. I associate this poem with Catholicism, which is something I feel I've escaped from. Guilt and shame are mentioned a lot.

It's very poignant at the end when he says, 'So I did sit and eat.' It expresses the idea of acceptance, of loving yourself, and I think that is the key to happiness – you can't give it out if you don't have it for yourself. All religions, I suppose, are about the attempt to get somebody to sit down, to love themselves in some way. The idea of love in its simplest form is what has allowed me, in a positive way, to reject Catholicism as a choice without denying me the right to be as kind, as loving and as grateful as any Catholic, because my God is that word, Love.

During the run of *Hamlet* at the Almeida Theatre, the word that I said in the wings every night before I went on was, 'Love'. It's a play about revenge and grief and murder, but essentially it's about people who are struggling to love each other or struggling to hate people that they actually love. I once heard someone say that the purpose of any art is to teach us how to live a better life, and to do that you've got to love in some way.

'Quick-eyed Love' is gorgeous. This idea that if you are Love, you're able in a second to see if somebody is upset or vulnerable, to see what they need.

Love (III)

Love bade me welcome. Yet my soul drew back
                    Guilty of dust and sin.
But quick-eyed Love, observing me grow slack
                    From my first entrance in,
Drew nearer to me, sweetly questioning,
                    If I lacked any thing.

A guest, I answered, worthy to be here:
                    Love said, You shall be he.
I the unkind, ungrateful? Ah my dear,
                    I cannot look on thee.
Love took my hand, and smiling did reply,
                    Who made the eyes but I?

Truth Lord, but I have marred them: let my shame
                    Go where it doth deserve.
And know you not, says Love, who bore the blame?
                    My dear, then I will serve.
You must sit down, says Love, and taste my meat:
                    So I did sit and eat.

George Herbert

Harbor Dawn *by* Lucy Maud Montgomery

The poem that's been a friend to Ann Lewis

For over six years, my friend Elizabeth and I have each shared a poem and an illustrative photo every day. Elizabeth is steeped in poetry and drama, and I love nature photography. It started with a chance exchange over a photo and is now a firm commitment that we maintain. The whole thing has become almost a ritual and as a result, I've learned so much about poetry. Elizabeth typically starts from a poem and finds an illustration. I often start with a photo.

In the autumn of 2017, I was lucky enough to witness and photograph a beautiful pink dawn in Penzance harbour in Cornwall. I looked for a poem and was blown away by Lucy Maud Montgomery's exquisite imagery. It brings a lump to my throat every time I read it; the last few lines of the first stanza are so achingly beautiful.

During the first lockdown in 2020, when we were confined to our local streets for walking, I often went out very early. One morning, the sky filled up with rosy wine again, and the poem came to mind straight away. I found myself reciting it in my head as I walked along. The pandemic turned everything we knew on its head, but the poem stuck with me. It has been a beacon of poetry's ability to express the sublime experience of nature at its most beautiful. It's guaranteed to brighten a dark day.

We've shared many poems over those six years, and I've fallen in love with lots of them. This one is still very special, and I love to share it when the autumn sunrises are gloriously pink and rosy.

Harbor Dawn

There's a hush and stillness calm and deep,
For the waves have wooed all the winds to sleep
In the shadow of headlands bold and steep;
But some gracious spirit has taken the cup
Of the crystal sky and filled it up
With rosy wine, and in it afar
Has dissolved the pearl of the morning star.

The girdling hills with the night-mist cold
In purple raiment are hooded and stoled
And smit on the brows with fire and gold;
And in the distance the wide, white sea
Is a thing of glamor and wizardry,
With its wild heart lulled to a passing rest,
And the sunrise cradled upon its breast.

With the first red sunlight on mast and spar
A ship is sailing beyond the bar,
Bound to a land that is fair and far;
And those who wait and those who go
Are brave and hopeful, for well they know
Fortune and favor the ship shall win
That crosses the bar when the dawn comes in.

Lucy Maud Montgomery

The Lake Isle of Innisfree *by* W. B. Yeats

The poem that's been a friend to Sue Lawther-Brown

This poem stopped me in my tracks when I first came across it. Every single word feels perfectly chosen and placed and so beautifully creates a sense of sanctuary.

It's not simply a safe space where nothing is happening. The poet is very specific – it's not finding a cabin but building it, planting the beans and looking after the bee hive – there's a very purposeful toil that is at the same time peaceful and deeply personal. It's so evocative and powerful, to 'live alone in the bee-loud glade' – that background hum that in the busyness of life you perhaps wouldn't notice, but here becomes so much more present.

At the time I encountered it, I was (and still am) working as a civil funeral celebrant. The strange thing is, all my life I've been afraid of death. There's a complicated but beautiful connection between a place of sanctuary and death, nature and life, wrapped up in this poem. Working as a celebrant has moved my thinking on and helped me become more at peace with the idea of death. This poem has been a really powerful part of that.

For me, this poem is almost like a jewel – it evokes something that I want to reach out and touch. That active choice expressed in the first line is really important to me – making a decision to go to this place of serenity. Sometimes you can feel things happening that are out of your control – they're going to impact you in some way and you don't quite know how. This poem just takes me to a place where I know it will be OK. I feel I want it close to me, as you would want a friend close to you when you need them.

The Lake Isle of Innisfree

I will arise and go now, and go to Innisfree,
And a small cabin build there, of clay and wattles made:
Nine bean-rows will I have there, a hive for the honey-bee;
And live alone in the bee-loud glade.

And I shall have some peace there, for peace comes
    dropping slow,
Dropping from the veils of the morning to where the
    cricket sings;
There midnight's all a glimmer, and noon a purple glow,
And evening full of the linnet's wings.

I will arise and go now, for always night and day
I hear lake water lapping with low sounds by the shore;
While I stand on the roadway, or on the pavements grey,
I hear it in the deep heart's core.

W. B. Yeats

The Negro Speaks of Rivers *by* Langston Hughes

The poem that's been a friend to Roy McFarlane

I first came across this poem in the late nineties, on my journey of Black identity. I'd been looking at readings from Black intellectuals, especially around the period they called the Harlem Renaissance. All these amazing poets and thinkers and artists of the 1920s in Harlem. Langston Hughes kept coming up. This was literally the first poem I found of his, and one of the first poems that entranced me, blew me away.

He had so much to say about the Negro person at that time. After coming through slavery, after Jim Crow and still being beaten down by society, police officers, poverty, he's there saying we have a journey too. We have been here, we need to be proud of who we are and we need to sing it out loud. He was only nineteen at the time he wrote this, such a wise head on young shoulders.

I was working as a mentor to young Black men. We were on a journey together – Who are we? What is it to be in this world? Langston Hughes was that friend, that brother by my side telling me that we are beautiful people, we don't have to be militant, we have to be angry, but we can still share our voice. He didn't shy away from the hard subjects, but he didn't just leave it there either. He was looking for a solution for how all of humanity could come together and make a difference. That's the thing that took hold of me and got me writing.

Discovering Hughes was a huge influence on my journey as a poet, how you can go deep and say so much in just a few lines. It wasn't about analysing it, it was just beautiful; song, praise. It was everything.

The Negro Speaks of Rivers

I've known rivers:
I've known rivers ancient as the world and older than
      the flow of human blood in human veins.

My soul has grown deep like the rivers.

I bathed in the Euphrates when dawns were young.
I built my hut near the Congo and it lulled me to sleep.
I looked upon the Nile and raised the pyramids above it.
I heard the singing of the Mississippi when Abe Lincoln
      went down to New Orleans, and I've seen its
      muddy bosom turn all golden in the sunset.

I've known rivers:
Ancient, dusky rivers.

My soul has grown deep like the rivers.

Langston Hughes

My Dark Horses *by* Jodie Hollander

The poem that's been a friend to Rosie Garland

Here is a poem with its doors open, leaving space in the conversation for the reader. It uses the image of a stable and horses and invites us to come in. The poem explores a sense of groundedness: however battered we feel, and however under threat the world seems, we can still find shelter.

The poem is a reminder of the importance of stillness. It creates a moment when we can choose to join the dark horses in the shed while the storm passes overhead. There will be storms but they won't, they can't, last forever. I like the way it shows how things aren't static, and nothing stays the same.

It's not suggesting a tinkly, twee calm. It's more considered and grounded. Neither is it passive because it involves engagement of the self. The poem does that in a very particular way, by invoking a sense of communion and community – this isn't about one horse, it's about all the horses.

We are living at a time when there's an increasing sense of fragmentation and isolation, and this poem reminds us that neither is helpful. It suggests an image of the friends and loved ones who surround us and how this mitigates against isolation. One of the ways we can take care of ourselves is to form communities. Although there is an 'I' in this poem, it's very much an 'I' in relation to others, and how important it is simply to stand close together.

This poem offers me a friend who is a good listener. Not flashy but quietly sure of themselves in a way that has been learned through experience. Someone who knows they can learn plenty more. We all deserve friends like that.

My Dark Horses

If only I were more like my dark horses,
I wouldn't have to worry all the time
that I was running too little and resting too much.
I'd spend my hours grazing in the sunlight,
taking long naps in the vast pastures.
And when it was time to move along I'd know;
I'd spend some time with all those that I'd loved,
then disappear into a gathering of trees.

If only I were more like my dark horses,
I wouldn't be so frightened of the storms;
instead, when the clouds began to gather and fill
I'd make my way calmly to the shed,
and stand close to all the other horses.
Together, we'd let the rain fall round us,
knowing as darkness passes overhead
that above all, this is the time to be still.

Jodie Hollander

On Wenlock Edge the wood's in trouble *by* A. E. Housman

The poem that's been a friend to Serena Trowbridge

I started reading A. E. Housman's poetry when I was about twenty. I really connected with it, perhaps because of his combination of nostalgia and melancholy, and in this poem, quite a lot of melodrama, which appealed to me.

I've always felt that to read a book was never enough – I had to live that book.

When you learn a poem by heart, you feel it, live it, know it – it becomes part of you. I learned this by heart. I'd wander around the fields muttering it to myself. I remember one time standing on a table in a pub declaiming it to people. I still feel like this poem is in me, and it's a poem I have shared with my son, who has also learned it by heart.

I've always been a bit obsessed with history and much more interested in people's everyday lives than in battles and monarchs. I enjoy thinking about how people have always felt certain things. For me it's about human connection, moments of continuity that often come across much better in poetry than in any other written form. This poem works so well partly because it is a specific and identifiable place, somewhere you feel you could go and be and literally channel these people. It expresses this idea that what we look at and what we feel, in nature as well as human nature, is unchanging in many ways. People have felt this before and the world has moved on, and you feel this now, and things will move on again. When I first read this poem, it brought all that together for me.

I feel like the narrator is speaking to me but also that I'm speaking back, constructing a dialogue in my head. It's familiar yet at times uncomfortable and challenging, in the way that conversations with good friends can be.

On Wenlock Edge the wood's in trouble

On Wenlock Edge the wood's in trouble;
    His forest fleece the Wrekin heaves;
The gale, it plies the saplings double,
    And thick on Severn snow the leaves.

'Twould blow like this through holt and hanger
    When Uricon the city stood:
'Tis the old wind in the old anger,
    But then it threshed another wood.

Then, 'twas before my time, the Roman
    At yonder heaving hill would stare:
The blood that warms an English yeoman,
    The thoughts that hurt him, they were there.

There, like the wind through woods in riot,
    Through him the gale of life blew high;
The tree of man was never quiet:
    Then 'twas the Roman, now 'tis I.

The gale, it plies the saplings double,
    It blows so hard, 'twill soon be gone:
To-day the Roman and his trouble
    Are ashes under Uricon.

A. E. Housman

Voyages II *by* Hart Crane

The poem that's been a friend to Subhadassi

I came across this poem when I was twenty-four and on a four-month Buddhist retreat in the Spanish mountains. It was spring, and the wild Spanish irises were in bloom and a whole variety of orchids carpeted the valley. During the retreat, along with twenty-five others, I was ordained. I was given the name 'Subhadassi', which means 'the one who finds beauty'.

As part of my ordination, I was given a Buddha visualization to help me connect more fully with the qualities of 'enlightenment' in an embodied way. This Buddha was the archetypal Buddha Amitabha, who is red in colour and associated with the ocean, the setting sun, and profound clarity. This poem seemed to invoke the presence of something very strongly connected to this Buddha, and to Buddhism itself. I would recite the poem in my own mind before I began meditation. It set the scene beautifully with its intense incantation and became a great friend in ushering me towards the heart of my Buddhist practice.

The poem has the strength and breadth of the ocean it describes, which perhaps is the ocean of life. The waves as thick silk sheets; the moon and the waters; the extraordinary poinsettias, which, in my imagination, became lotuses that Amitabha the red Buddha held and that the Buddha sat upon. These in turn were the 'floating flowers' in the poem that close round with 'sleep, death, desire'. This image perfectly counterpoints the ending with its open resonance, where nothing is pinned down and the richness of our existential situation is evoked.

This intense relationship went on for a few years; I wrapped myself in its sonic power, its incantatory realm, and found succour in it. Now, thirty years or so later, it has returned to my mind more fully, as has the red Buddha.

Voyages II

—And yet this great wink of eternity,
Of rimless floods, unfettered leewardings,
Samite sheeted and processioned where
Her undinal vast belly moonward bends,
Laughing the wrapt inflections of our love;

Take this Sea, whose diapason knells
On scrolls of silver snowy sentences,
The sceptred terror of whose sessions rends
As her demeanors motion well or ill,
All but the pieties of lovers' hands.

And onward, as bells off San Salvador
Salute the crocus lustres of the stars,
In these poinsettia meadows of her tides,—
Adagios of islands, O my Prodigal,
Complete the dark confessions her veins spell.

Mark how her turning shoulders wind the hours,
And hasten while her penniless rich palms
Pass superscription of bent foam and wave,—
Hasten, while they are true,—sleep, death, desire,
Close round one instant in one floating flower.

Bind us in time, O Seasons clear, and awe.
O minstrel galleons of Carib fire,
Bequeath us to no earthly shore until
Is answered in the vortex of our grave
The seal's wide spindrift gaze toward paradise.

Hart Crane

(What Survives) *by* Rainer Maria Rilke *tr. A. Poulin, Jr.*

The poem that's been a friend to Lois P. Jones

From the very first moment of reading Rilke I experienced this aliveness in his poetry. It was not at all like communing with a dead poet. Here was this voice, so intimate and so luminous it made me feel his presence.

I love poems that invite me to return to them. I have this one posted on my little billboard at work, and new insights still come to me every time I refer to it. That's what gives an apparently little poem such significance. It's almost as if the poem continues to grow. It keeps on working; it keeps doing something in the world, inside you, the reader.

The idea of what continues, what stays after we go is important to me. The opening line is so beautiful and arresting. The way Rilke advances his ideas, from one thought to another, surprises and excites me. He moves on to explore how anything can change, that things transform and we are not fixed by what's happened to us. The image of the battle, to me, is to do with the physical and non-physical realms, our existence in this world as spiritual beings. It's the ultimate idea of the continuation of the soul, how things can transform and transcend, and continue to be and continue to grow.

There's a tenderness and a sensuality in Rilke's way, in his being, in his work. How seductive is that? No wonder so many women fell for him, and men too. For me, it was like meeting a soul friend. Someone once said, 'A good poem is a mystery you can trust,' and so it is for me with this poem. Even though I can't pin down every inch of it, I trust what's underneath.

(What Survives)

Who says that all must vanish?
Who knows, perhaps the flight
of the bird you wound remains,
and perhaps flowers survive
caresses in us, in their ground.

It isn't the gesture that lasts,
but it dresses you again in gold
armor —from breast to knees—
and the battle was so pure
an Angel wears it after you.

Rainer Maria Rilke
tr. A. Poulin, Jr.

The Friend that

Helps Me Wrestle

with the

Difficult Things

The Guest House *by* Rumi *tr. Coleman Barks*

The poem that's been a friend to Yasmin Ali

I have this poem on the wall facing my bed, so it's the first thing I see. It's a good message to start the day off with.

It reminds me to be present, to go through the day attentively, and take in as much as I can. It ties in well with how I live my life on the basis of my religion as a Muslim. The very first line tells us that this world is temporary and ever-changing. It's not everything and there is another life beyond this realm.

'Be grateful for whoever comes, / because each has been sent as a guide from beyond.' This line reminds me of a verse in the Quran, which roughly translates as 'verily with hardship comes ease'. No matter what happens, something good will come afterwards. Each person you meet can teach you something and you can teach them something. We believe that when things happen that are particularly hard, or frightening, or tragic, God wouldn't give you that experience unless you could handle it and grow from it.

Being born in Liverpool to Somali parents who came here during the civil war, being a Muslim woman, a Scouser: there's a lot to deal with. In the past I would bury difficult things. When the media constantly puts you in a box – or politicians tell you that you're a terrorist and you're not welcome in this country – you grow up questioning your beliefs and your identity. It's important for your mental health not to bottle things up. I've found a way, partly with the help of this poem, to acknowledge when things are affecting me, to look at them and simply evaluate how I can move forward.

It is a warm, non-judgemental friend that sees every aspect of the issue and comforts you when you need it most.

The Guest House

This being human is a guest house.
Every morning a new arrival.

A joy, a depression, a meanness,
some momentary awareness comes
as an unexpected visitor.

Welcome and entertain them all!
Even if they're a crowd of sorrows,
who violently sweep your house
empty of its furniture,
still, treat each guest honorably.
He may be clearing you out
for some new delight.

The dark thought, the shame, the malice,
meet them at the door laughing,
and invite them in.

Be grateful for whoever comes,
because each has been sent
as a guide from beyond.

Rumi
tr. Coleman Barks

Turns *by* Tony Harrison

The poem that's been a friend to Maxine Peake

My grandad always wore a cap, so initially that was what spoke to me in this poem. We had a great relationship, and he was a massive influence on me. He was in the Communist Party, was self-educated and worked at Leyland Motors. He wouldn't leave the house without his cap on.

The imagery here is about working-class identity and how it will hold you back. When I first read this poem, I was determined that it wouldn't, because I was going to drama school in London and would leave it all behind. I was eighteen and had this attitude that I was too big for this place. When I got to RADA one of the teachers said to me, 'When you go back it will be very difficult for you, and you won't feel like you fit any more.' In fact, I found that I needed to come home and see my friends.

This poem carries some of the strange relationship I have with my class and which I've let be my identity sometimes. It can be a bit suffocating because people put 'northern' before anything you are or do. It's a love/hate thing.

I've got lots of labels and sometimes I do feel weighed down by them, but at the same time I don't want to be someone who doesn't speak out. A friend of mine said to me, 'I think you've taken on your grandad's role and now he's gone, you feel that you have to take it all on.'

I love that image of the initials inside the cap. I can see it, the little patch inside with the plastic, a bit oily from the Brylcreem. I've still got my grandad's cap. It still smells of him.

It's not exactly a gentle friend, this poem. Some friendships aren't always comforting, but the important ones remind you of what you need to hear.

Turns

I thought it made me look more 'working class'
(as if a bit of chequered cloth could bridge that gap!)
I did a turn in it before the glass.
My mother said: It suits you, your dad's cap.
(She preferred me to wear suits and part my hair:
You're every bit as good as that lot are!)

All the pension queue came out to stare.
Dad was sprawled beside the postbox (still VR),
his cap turned inside up beside his head,
smudged H A H in purple Indian ink
and Brylcreem slicks displayed so folks might think
he wanted charity for dropping dead.

He never begged. For nowt! Death's reticence
crowns his life, and me, I'm opening my trap
to busk the class that broke him for the pence
that splash like brackish tears into our cap.

Tony Harrison

Proem *by* Martin Carter

The poem that's been a friend to Nicholas Laughlin

This poem is a riddle; every time you read it the meaning seems to shift a little bit. I like the fact that I can only tell you what this poem is by reading it out loud, and imagining how it came to be in the mind of the person who wrote it.

Certainly in Guyana, Martin Carter's words and lines have entered the public imagination. People can quote him the way they quote Shakespeare – he just trips off the tongue. There are many of Carter's lines that so exactly fit a certain dilemma in our everyday lives that we quote him almost without realizing it.

The poem itself is this sinuous reaching down that mimics the action of tree roots, snaking down, probing away and investigating the subterranean or maybe even the subconscious. Then the leaves up in the sun – these two different processes of being buried, or being up in the open air.

We don't understand a lot of what happens to us. This is a poem about the fact that perhaps comprehension is not a state, it's a process. We never get to a fixed point of saying, 'I understand this, I grasp this' – it's always in the present continuous, it's never-ending. As I get older, there is a comfort in this poem, in accepting that everything won't always make sense and that perhaps not comprehending is the point.

If I were told that the planet was about to explode and I could take one poem with me to the rocket ship – this might be the one I grabbed. In the depths of space, I could continue reading it for many years, and this inexhaustible poem would continue to intrigue me.

Proem

Not, in the saying of you, are you
said. Baffled and like a root
stopped by a stone you turn back questioning
the tree you feed. But what the leaves hear
is not what the roots ask. Inexhaustibly,
being at one time what was to be said
and at another time what has been said
the saying of you remains the living of you
never to be said. But, enduring,
you change with the change that changes
and yet are not of the changing of any of you.
Ever yourself, you are always about
to be yourself in something else ever with me.

Martin Carter

Diving into the Wreck *by* Adrienne Rich

The poem that's been a friend to Andrea Witzke Slot

I was in grad school, in my early thirties, when I first read this poem. The other students were younger than me and I was coming to it a bit further into life, as a mother and some-one going through a divorce. Adrienne Rich was also going through a period of immense change when she wrote this poem. She had been married and raised children; then, after her husband died, she met the love of her life, another woman.

The line that really gets me is, 'the wreck and not the story of the wreck / the thing itself and not the myth'. She's saying, here's the water – some of you are going to stay above it, relying on the myths and stories other people have told you, the stories that structure our lives. Below it, there is this world that's unknown, murky, maybe ugly, maybe beautiful too – that's exciting, but also frightening. There's a ladder, and it's always there and we might just dip our toe in, or we might put on the wetsuit, get the tank and jump in.

The extended metaphor of diving was so powerful for me as a woman writer and academic – this idea of entering places that had been inhabited by men for years. I've always believed that we need to have the courage to look at those things that really hurt and make us feel uncomfortable in order to grow. So this poem spoke to me about my own relationships and beginning life on my own, as a single mother and as a writer finding my way.

It's the friend who wants to talk about the more difficult things. She challenges me. She says, 'Andrea, you'd better look hard. Are you carrying that knife? Are you willing to go down another rung on the ladder?'

Diving into the Wreck

First having read the book of myths,
and loaded the camera,
and checked the edge of the knife-blade,
I put on
the body-armor of black rubber
the absurd flippers
the grave and awkward mask.
I am having to do this
not like Cousteau with his
assiduous team
aboard the sun-flooded schooner
but here alone.

There is a ladder.
The ladder is always there
hanging innocently
close to the side of the schooner.
We know what it is for,
we who have used it.
Otherwise
it is a piece of maritime floss
some sundry equipment.

I go down.
Rung after rung and still
the oxygen immerses me
the blue light
the clear atoms
of our human air.
I go down.
My flippers cripple me,
I crawl like an insect down the ladder

and there is no one
to tell me when the ocean
will begin.

First the air is blue and then
it is bluer and then green and then
black I am blacking out and yet
my mask is powerful
it pumps my blood with power
the sea is another story
the sea is not a question of power
I have to learn alone
to turn my body without force
in the deep element.

And now: it is easy to forget
what I came for
among so many who have always
lived here
swaying their crenellated fans
between the reefs
and besides
you breathe differently down here.

I came to explore the wreck.
The words are purposes.
The words are maps.
I came to see the damage that was done
and the treasures that prevail.
I stroke the beam of my lamp
slowly along the flank
of something more permanent
than fish or weed

the thing I came for:
the wreck and not the story of the wreck
the thing itself and not the myth

the drowned face always staring
toward the sun
the evidence of damage
worn by salt and sway into this threadbare beauty
the ribs of the disaster
curving their assertion
among the tentative haunters.

This is the place.
And I am here, the mermaid whose dark hair
streams black, the merman in his armored body.
We circle silently
about the wreck
we dive into the hold.
I am she: I am he

whose drowned face sleeps with open eyes
whose breasts still bear the stress
whose silver, copper, vermeil cargo lies
obscurely inside barrels
half-wedged and left to rot
we are the half-destroyed instruments
that once held to a course
the water-eaten log
the fouled compass

We are, I am, you are
by cowardice or courage
the one who find our way
back to this scene
carrying a knife, a camera
a book of myths
in which
our names do not appear.

Adrienne Rich

On Children *by* Kahlil Gibran

The poem that's been a friend to Hafsah Aneela Bashir

After I'd had children, I went back to study and did English Literature and criminology. We covered the traditional English literary canon. After I finished my degree, I felt that I needed something more. Partly because of my spirituality and my faith as a Muslim, I found myself drawn to a number of Eastern poets that were part of my heritage. Arab literature is a lot softer on my heart and my head.

I've got five children: the youngest is eight, the oldest twenty-one. Suddenly the older ones were off to uni, doing their own thing, and I really didn't want them to leave. I felt a rejection, which I knew was silly, but it was real. It sent me into turmoil.

A few years back, a friend of mine had given me Kahlil Gibran's *The Prophet*. I hadn't really connected with it at the time, but when these feelings arose, I went back to this poem and it really guided me. 'Your children are not your children.' They are not possessions. If I could, I'd keep them forever, but this poem reminds me that you can't do that. You can guide them as much as you want but ultimately, they are their own person.

Bringing up five individuals in this world is a big responsibility. This poem helps to lighten the weight of that. Gibran gives us this wonderful image of the archer and the bow. There is stability to the bow, but it can bend in the archer's hand. It helped me realize that being rigid is not always the best way.

They're so independent now. It's just like living with housemates. We've got to that stage where we pass each other on the stairs and think, I've seen you somewhere before.

On Children

Your children are not your children.
They are the sons and daughters of Life's longing for itself.
They come through you but not from you,
And though they are with you yet they belong not to you.

You may give them your love but not your thoughts,
For they have their own thoughts.
You may house their bodies but not their souls,
For their souls dwell in the house of tomorrow,
which you cannot visit, not even in your dreams.
You may strive to be like them,
but seek not to make them like you.
For life goes not backward nor tarries with yesterday.

You are the bows from which your children
as living arrows are sent forth.
The archer sees the mark upon the path of the infinite,
and He bends you with His might
that His arrows may go swift and far.
Let your bending in the archer's hand be for gladness;
For even as He loves the arrow that flies,
so He loves also the bow that is stable.

Kahlil Gibran

Truth *by* Jean 'Binta' Breeze

The poem that's been a friend to Sue Brown

I love the way Jean writes, her use of the Jamaican language and the English language, song, movement, and the vibrations of all of those elements. Between each word and line, you know that other things are going on.

The poem invites us to ask – what is truth? For many women, there are expectations about how we should live and present ourselves in a certain way. So what resonates for me here in the strength of this story is the integrity of the position she is taking – you do what you have to do, I'm going to do it my way.

She is claiming her identity and freedom on her own terms. She is going to 'live simply without even a bed' – stories are her wealth. Who I am and what I've learned and gained, the pains and joys, it's all here and I'm ready to share it. The key is that she's sharing this wealth – these stories – with children. She knows that they are growing up in a world where distraction is the main thing and with forms of education that take you away from what you need to know. They are the next generation, and she is offering them her truth.

It resonates with me especially because of my dad. With him, everything was a story. For that generation the oral tradition was a vital thing; to impart their experiences to us as children, to share their knowledge and doubts. I loved the theatrics of it, the drama, and the richness of the language.

This phrase, 'give her voice to the wind'. It's not restricted or held down; the wind carries it out there into the universe and it will seep into the minds of those young ones who are listening.

Truth

some years after
when the laughter came again
she grew her hair in locks around her head
and lived
simply
without even a bed   but she

she had stories   that woman
she had stories to tell
and children who listened   well
and she
she hid nothing
made no excuses for self

just let
truth give her voice to the wind

and she would sing sometimes   sing and
ask a little more time
for memory to swell their heads

the children gathered around her
the more they asked
the more words she was sent
words that crossed all ages
served no laws
words that questioned all they had been taught

so they put her away
one day
she must be mad
the adults say
corrupting young minds
it's obvious   depraved

she grew silent then
her laughter grew thin
then left with the wind

but the children grew up and remembered
one woman who didn't lie
one woman who didn't hide

now they count the hypocrites around them

Jean 'Binta' Breeze

Postscript *by* Seamus Heaney

The poem that's been a friend to Clem Burrows

I first read this poem in *100 Poems*, a posthumous collection of Heaney's work put together after his death by his family. 'Postscript' is placed towards the end.

I was sent the collection by a dear friend at a time when I was spinning more plates than I could handle, and also going through an upheaval in my personal life. Things were getting tricky and I was afraid of losing my grip. When I read 'Postscript' I had a palpable sense of being spoken to directly by Seamus Heaney, in a visceral encounter. He has been a touchstone poet for me all my life, but never before had I experienced such a direct hit.

It's a magnificent poem – the beat and shape of the poem is in harmony with its subject, the buffeting of life and the quest for peace. To start a poem with 'And' is audacious, yet it's gentle too, easing you into the poem's journey that is both physical and emotional. I remember feeling arrested by that opening line, its instruction, and then utterly gut-punched by the ending. You anticipate some solace from this invitation to take a drive out into nature and all the brilliant detail he gives you – the shore, the lake, the swans and the light – but then he comes at you with this extra challenge at the end. He's saying, there is no way to hold on to this place of perspective. It's an energizing salve he's offering, not a passive one. I love that.

The title is apt for many reasons; it's acknowledging that we tend to forget to take a moment, to reflect, get perspective. Placed towards the end of this posthumous book, it's a sense for me that Heaney will always be there, offering me his insight, his P.S.

Postscript

And some time make the time to drive out west
Into County Clare, along the Flaggy Shore,
In September or October, when the wind
And the light are working off each other
So that the ocean on one side is wild
With foam and glitter, and inland among stones
The surface of a slate-grey lake is lit
By the earthed lightning of a flock of swans,
Their feathers roughed and ruffling, white on white,
Their fully grown headstrong-looking heads
Tucked or cresting or busy underwater.
Useless to think you'll park and capture it
More thoroughly. You are neither here nor there,
A hurry through which known and strange things pass
As big soft buffetings come at the car sideways
And catch the heart off guard and blow it open.

Seamus Heaney

Ashes of Life *by* Edna St. Vincent Millay

The poem that's been a friend to Laura Wade

One long, hot summer in my late twenties, I was busy falling in love in a completely distracting and debilitating way. It was a time of huge intensity. For quite a long time it wasn't clear whether my feelings were going to be requited, so I was in this weird love limbo. My attention span dwindled to almost nothing because I was so busy thinking about him, but poetry I could manage, because it was shorter and could hold me. I remember how deeply comforting this poem was at that point. It's direct and feels very modern.

Although it's about the end of a love affair, it spoke to my situation because in some way I was preparing myself for the fact that this relationship might not happen. I knew that if it didn't, it would take me a long time to get over it. Some of the intensity I was experiencing was reflected back to me in Millay's writing. There's a restlessness of spirit here but also an endurance – agony as a thing that has to be got through. I remember taking long 'thinky' walks and reciting it to myself. It has a carrying on to it, a 'keep walking' encouragement. The rhyme supports that, a feeling that the line will be completed – we will get through this.

Despite all the grief and pain, the poem has a heartbeat that will continue, life is going on. 'Tomorrow and tomorrow and tomorrow and tomorrow'. I love how she does four of them – like she's taking Shakespeare on and raising him one.

For me, poetry is that friend I feel guilty about because I only ring them when I'm having a crisis, and actually I should seek them out for a nice cosy dinner on a day when nothing terrible has gone wrong.

Ashes of Life

Love has gone and left me and the days are all alike;
   Eat I must, and sleep I will, — and would that night were here!
But ah! — to lie awake and hear the slow hours strike!
   Would that it were day again! — with twilight near!

Love has gone and left me and I don't know what to do;
   This or that or what you will is all the same to me;
But all the things that I begin I leave before I'm through, —
   There's little use in anything as far as I can see.

Love has gone and left me, — and the neighbors knock and borrow,
   And life goes on forever like the gnawing of a mouse, —
And tomorrow and tomorrow and tomorrow and tomorrow
   There's this little street and this little house.

Edna St. Vincent Millay

How The World Gets Bigger *by* Alyson Hallett

The poem that's been a friend to Roxy Dunn

This poem was part of a leaflet tucked inside a card my mum sent me when I first moved to London. The leaflet contained lots of poems, and I cut this one out and stuck it on my wall – it was there for six years.

I'm drawn to writing that takes you from a place of difficulty towards something enlightening, or comforting, or hopeful. I'm quite open to feeling sad in order to feel happy again. You need to face the sadness and accept it before you can move on and be more positive.

In the poem someone is facing rejection, maybe emotional, maybe a career thing. 'This is better than crying' – I've always loved that line. The rain, just pouring down and crying for you, its tears are bigger than yours. Rain has that really cathartic feeling, like the big emotional release you get when crying. At the end there's an astonishing moment of hope: 'the corner at the end of the road suddenly appealing, the way it turns without revealing what lies beyond.' For me it's about picking yourself up, moving forward, the idea that however bad you may feel in this moment, if you turn the corner there's promise.

When I don't know what to say to a friend in a moment of crisis, I try to find poems that say something for me. I sent this poem to a friend who'd broken up with her boyfriend. 'How The World Gets Bigger': even the title is saying to us, remember, as one thing closes another opens.

How The World Gets Bigger

This morning there's a note pinned to your door
explaining why you've had to rush out
and cancel our meeting. I turn back into
the rain, watch it falling on tarmac, rivering
in gutters, little bullets exploding. I unbutton
my jacket, lift my face to the sky. This is better
than crying; nowhere to be and nothing to do.
I walk the christened pavement, cherry tree
hung like a chandelier, the corner at the end
of the road suddenly appealing, the way it
turns without revealing what lies beyond.

Alyson Hallett

Ode to a Nightingale *by* John Keats

The poem that's been a friend to Brittany Grech

I remember going to a second-hand market with my parents, on the coast in Australia, when I was fourteen, and an old dusty book in a $2 toolbox caught my eye. I was attracted to its old book smell and lime green cover. It was an anthology called *A Galaxy of Poems Old and New*. I knew instantly I had to buy it, and I used my pocket money to get it.

Later that day as we were driving along the coast, the rolling cliffs and glistening seas at my window, I flipped through my book and came across the poem 'Ode to a Nightingale'.

From the first line I was completely immersed. After I read each stanza, my heart skipped a beat, I would gaze out of the window and intermittently let out sighs. From that moment on, my life and relationship with poetry changed forever!

I was bullied a lot in school and Keats was my escape. Poetry was my go-to place. This line reminds me of that: 'That I might drink, and leave the world unseen, / And with thee fade away into the forest dim'. When the words were hurtful at school, Keats's words would comfort me. 'Forlorn! the very word is like a bell / To toll me back from thee to my sole self!' It reminded me of the helplessness I felt. It resonated with the back and forth of my feelings and behaviours, how things affected me as opposed to how they affected those who did the bullying.

This poem will always be a dear friend to me; to this day it gives me hope in tricky times. Most of all this poem is forever my reminder to be kind and loving, to be romantic and to embrace the beauty that is around us!

Ode to a Nightingale

My heart aches, and a drowsy numbness pains
    My sense, as though of hemlock I had drunk,
Or emptied some dull opiate to the drains
    One minute past, and Lethe-wards had sunk:
'Tis not through envy of thy happy lot,
    But being too happy in thine happiness,—
        That thou, light-winged Dryad of the trees
          In some melodious plot
    Of beechen green, and shadows numberless,
        Singest of summer in full-throated ease.

O, for a draught of vintage! that hath been
    Cool'd a long age in the deep-delved earth,
Tasting of Flora and the country green,
    Dance, and Provençal song, and sunburnt mirth!
O for a beaker full of the warm South,
    Full of the true, the blushful Hippocrene,
        With beaded bubbles winking at the brim,
          And purple-stained mouth;
    That I might drink, and leave the world unseen,
        And with thee fade away into the forest dim:

Fade far away, dissolve, and quite forget
    What thou among the leaves hast never known,
The weariness, the fever, and the fret
    Here, where men sit and hear each other groan;
Where palsy shakes a few, sad, last gray hairs,
    Where youth grows pale, and spectre-thin, and dies;
        Where but to think is to be full of sorrow
          And leaden-eyed despairs,
    Where Beauty cannot keep her lustrous eyes,
        Or new Love pine at them beyond to-morrow.

Away! away! for I will fly to thee,
    Not charioted by Bacchus and his pards,
But on the viewless wings of Poesy,
    Though the dull brain perplexes and retards:
Already with thee! tender is the night,
    And haply the Queen-Moon is on her throne,
        Cluster'd around by all her starry Fays;
            But here there is no light,
    Save what from heaven is with the breezes blown
        Through verdurous glooms and winding mossy ways.

I cannot see what flowers are at my feet,
    Nor what soft incense hangs upon the boughs,
But, in embalmed darkness, guess each sweet
    Wherewith the seasonable month endows
The grass, the thicket, and the fruit-tree wild;
    White hawthorn, and the pastoral eglantine;
        Fast fading violets cover'd up in leaves;
            And mid-May's eldest child,
    The coming musk-rose, full of dewy wine,
        The murmurous haunt of flies on summer eves.

Darkling I listen; and, for many a time
    I have been half in love with easeful Death,
Call'd him soft names in many a mused rhyme,
    To take into the air my quiet breath;
Now more than ever seems it rich to die,
    To cease upon the midnight with no pain,
        While thou art pouring forth thy soul abroad
            In such an ecstasy!
    Still wouldst thou sing, and I have ears in vain—
        To thy high requiem become a sod.

Thou wast not born for death, immortal Bird!
    No hungry generations tread thee down;
The voice I hear this passing night was heard
    In ancient days by emperor and clown:
Perhaps the self-same song that found a path
      Through the sad heart of Ruth, when, sick for home,
        She stood in tears amid the alien corn;
          The same that oft-times hath
    Charm'd magic casements, opening on the foam
      Of perilous seas, in faery lands forlorn.

Forlorn! the very word is like a bell
    To toll me back from thee to my sole self!
Adieu! the fancy cannot cheat so well
    As she is fam'd to do, deceiving elf.
Adieu! adieu! thy plaintive anthem fades
    Past the near meadows, over the still stream,
      Up the hill-side; and now 'tis buried deep
        In the next valley-glades:
    Was it a vision, or a waking dream?
      Fled is that music:—Do I wake or sleep?

John Keats

The Friend that
Names
My Experience

Prayer *by* Carol Ann Duffy

The poem that's been a friend to Tricia Waller

This is a poem about how difficult life is and how you're on your own. There are a lot of sounds in it – the birdsong, piano, radio. You don't even realize it, but they're like prayers. When I was little we lived near the railway line, so the trains remind me of my childhood, as does the shipping forecast – I used to listen to that with my dad. It reminds me of being little and feeling safe. People can let you down, but these little sounds, they're constant, reliable.

Stanza three is the part that really gets to me. 'Someone calls / a child's name as though they named their loss.' I lost my first child. Where is he? I don't know. That line is calling his name. I've never been able to find him and probably never will. So that's for him. You come through it, because we're humans and we have to come through it, but of course, it's still there, it's still with you.

I lost my religion when I lost my child. I tried to fool myself I was OK, nothing could touch me, but it was a lie. Carol Ann Duffy and this poem intervened; she introduced this other form of prayer. The sieve of the hands, it's such a powerful image – it captures that moment when you don't know what to do, so you just cradle your head in your hands.

This is a constant friend. I can go to this poem and know someone else sees me and her words are still there, and she's still sincere enough to mean those words to me.

Prayer

Some days, although we cannot pray, a prayer
utters itself. So, a woman will lift
her head from the sieve of her hands and stare
at the minims sung by a tree, a sudden gift.

Some nights, although we are faithless, the truth
enters our hearts, that small familiar pain;
then a man will stand stock-still, hearing his youth
in the distant Latin chanting of a train.

Pray for us now. Grade 1 piano scales
console the lodger looking out across
a Midlands town. Then dusk, and someone calls
a child's name as though they named their loss.

Darkness outside. Inside, the radio's prayer -
Rockall. Malin. Dogger. Finisterre.

Carol Ann Duffy

5AM *by* Roxy Dunn

The poem that's been a friend to Paterson Joseph

Roxy Dunn is the poet who has awakened me to poetry in a new way and made me feel welcome.

This poem feels to me like your first lucid thought in the morning. You haven't quite closed the curtains and so the light wakes you up at 5 a.m. You're still under the covers resisting the urge to wake up. It's that vulnerable time when you're totally open to whatever might come. That's the place where you're going to get that nugget of a genius thought, or clarity about what you really want or need to do.

Whenever I read this poem, it's like I've just walked into a conversation and suddenly I see the world slightly differently. The ordinary made to look extraordinary. There's a profundity of thinking underneath her observations of everyday objects. Poetry as a way of thinking about the world.

When I was about thirteen, I used to bunk off school and go to the Willesden Green library. I'd hide out there and just read, read, read. I drank it in like it was life's blood. I'd walk the streets of Willesden, Cricklewood, Kilburn with a book in my hand in the way people do with their phones now. Words. Lots of them, couldn't get enough. Then when I went to drama school, poetry became something that you read with that funny voice you felt you had to put on – it ruined it for me. I can do all that, it's part of my skill, but when I want to be moved by something, I want it to be real.

This poem doesn't sell me flowers. It's not trying to paint the world in any other way than it is, but at the same time, it's not bleak. It's honest. A truthful friend. There's comfort in that.

5AM

It's not quite light
am I getting old?
old people wake early
half a croissant is on the desk
like a squashed crescent
and there's that record I bought
with the Soviet rocket sleeve

Around the corner in Highbury
Keith's cat has given you fleas
your bags are packed for Antibes
I wonder if I care about the right things
like rabbits dying slowly and Brexit
sometimes I'm secretly unfazed
I feel selfish and middle-aged

I'd like to play this rocket record
but I don't have a record player
the band are from Leeds, is that cool?
I can't work out if this is regret
or just the onset of dullness
I think I'll eat breakfast then sleep till noon
eat the remains of last night's moon

Roxy Dunn

Restlessness *by* D. H. Lawrence

The poem that's been a friend to Alison McManus

This poem speaks to something quite secret in me – 'Restlessness', a feeling I've had all my life. I've lived in different countries and always travelled, but now I'm married with children and I live and work in the same place. I never intended to stay for so many years.

One day, I went to Google and typed in 'restlessness poem'. This is what came up. I cried. Tears of recognition, I suppose. Just the imagery of this man in his room feeling trapped and lonely and wanting to connect with someone else, going out into the rain and looking at the faces of people as they walk past, wondering if they will see something in him, see his soul.

The umbrellas – people covering up, trying to protect themselves from an intense experience of life and nature and passion. That's part of the frustration for me, that sometimes you want to say, let's get rid of all that and just meet each other in an unguarded way, without barriers, without those umbrellas.

I have this pebble in my shoe sometimes, wanting to wander off. I would never leave my family, and yet sometimes you've got to stand in the window, feel the rain on your face and know that the night is out there. This poem acknowledges my feelings and reminds me they are temporary, and that in the morning when I wake up and look at my sons, my family and what I've created with them, I'm not going to feel restless any more.

I need to know this poem is here for me. It's that friend that gives you permission to feel the things that can be socially unacceptable and difficult to acknowledge.

Restlessness

At the open door of the room I stand and look at the night,
Hold my hand to catch the raindrops, that slant into sight,
Arriving grey from the darkness above suddenly into the light
      of the room.
I will escape from the hollow room, the box of light,
And be out in the bewildering darkness, which is always fecund,
      which might
Mate my hungry soul with a germ of its womb.

I will go out to the night, as a man goes down to the shore
To draw his net through the surf's thin line, at the dawn before
The sun warms the sea, little, lonely and sad, sifting the
      sobbing tide.
I will sift the surf that edges the night, with my net, the four
Strands of my eyes and my lips and my hands and my feet,
      sifting the store
Of flotsam until my soul is tired or satisfied.

I will catch in my eyes' quick net
The faces of all the women as they go past,
Bend over them with my soul, to cherish the wet
Cheeks and wet hair a moment, saying: 'Is it you?'
Looking earnestly under the dark umbrellas, held fast
Against the wind; and if, where the lamplight blew
Its rainy swill about us, she answered me
With a laugh and a merry wildness that it was she
Who was seeking me, and had found me at last to free
Me now from the stunting bonds of my chastity,
How glad I should be!

Moving along in the mysterious ebb of the night
Pass the men whose eyes are shut like anemones in a
      dark pool;
Why don't they open with vision and speak to me? what
      have they in sight?
Why do I wander aimless among them, desirous fool?

I can always linger over the huddled books on the stalls,
Always gladden my amorous fingers with the touch of
      their leaves,
Always kneel in courtship to the shelves in the doorways,
      where falls
The shadow, always offer myself to one mistress, who
      always receives.

But oh, it is not enough, it is all no good.
There is something I want to feel in my running blood,
Something I want to touch; I must hold my face to the rain,
I must hold my face to the wind, and let it explain
Me its life as it hurries in secret.
I will trail my hands again through the drenched, cold leaves
Till my hands are full of the chillness and touch of leaves,
Till at length they induce me to sleep, and to forget.

D. H. Lawrence

Love After Love *by* Derek Walcott

The poem that's been a friend to Jane Edington

I was sitting quietly with a dear friend who was enquiring into some aspects of my being. She listened patiently, then responded by reciting 'Love after Love'. She spoke Derek Walcott's words in such a way that I could feel them slipping through my normal conditioned reactions to reach a part of me that could really receive and accept them as pertinent to me. It was one of those moments when the world seemed to stop on its axis, as if all the 'pixels' that have made up my being flew around and imperceptibly rearranged themselves in a profoundly different form. I emerged with a belief that I had full right and responsibility to inhabit my existence on the earth and this was of value. The veils of conditioning and habit lifted entirely in that moment, and even the question of value didn't exist; it was inherent. I am so grateful for this poem.

Right from the start, 'The time will come when, with elation / you will greet yourself arriving at your own door' evokes a hopeful inevitability and invites a separation that can then lead to union. 'You will love again'. The 'again' gives me the quiet certainty that I will connect with that love and on I go! There really isn't any part of it that doesn't speak to me. The poem is short and exquisitely simple, yet complex at the same time. The words are etched on my mind. It ends simply – 'Sit. Feast on your life.' I am doing just that.

Love After Love

The time will come
when, with elation
you will greet yourself arriving
at your own door, in your own mirror
and each will smile at the other's welcome,

and say, sit here. Eat.
You will love again the stranger who was your self.
Give wine. Give bread. Give back your heart
to itself, to the stranger who has loved you

all your life, whom you ignored
for another, who knows you by heart.
Take down the love letters from the bookshelf,

the photographs, the desperate notes,
peel your own image from the mirror.
Sit. Feast on your life.

Derek Walcott

In My Country *by* Jackie Kay

The poem that's been a friend to Degna Stone

I remember the first time I read this poem; it was really powerful. Growing up in the eighties as a Black person, there was always that question, 'Where are you from?' and you would tell them, 'I'm from the Midlands,' and they would say, 'But where are you really from?' Finding a poem that so vividly creates that scene meant I could place myself in the poem.

It's not the question itself. It's cumulative, a kind of drip, drip, drip. There's not always an unpleasant intent behind it. Sometimes people are genuinely interested, and you have to bite down that anger at being asked this question that questions your validity. The validity of you being where you are, who you are.

I grew up on a council estate in Tamworth; I used to call myself a pseudo goth – I couldn't quite do the pale and interesting, but I had the black chiffon shirts and the German para boots. I felt very much like a British indie kid. That was part of my identity. When somebody asks, 'Where do you come from?' it displaces you, others you. That's what makes the last line of the poem so potent: '"Here," I said, "Here. These parts."'

It's an intensely political poem that talks about racialization and identity and belonging in a subtle way. It articulates something that is hard to communicate to people who've never experienced prejudice or racism. It's in the way people look at you sometimes that's hard to pinpoint. You feel it – a sense of dislike, suspicion, that 'slow watchful circle / as if I were a superstition'. The poem makes that feeling easier to bear. You know you're not on your own, you're not imagining it, you're not having a disproportionate response.

It gives me resolve. It's an unapologetic 'here I am'. It's the sort of friend that would get a group of you together and take you all on a protest.

In My Country

walking by the waters,
down where an honest river
shakes hands with the sea,
a woman passed round me
in a slow watchful circle
as if I were a superstition;

or the worst dregs of her imagination,
so when she finally spoke
her words spliced into bars
of an old wheel. A segment of air.
Where do you come from?
'Here,' I said, 'Here. These parts.'

Jackie Kay

When I was a Bird *by* Katherine Mansfield

The poem that's been a friend to Sarah Salway

My daughter once banned me from talking about my childhood because apparently, I came across as such a 'lonely loser'.

I was amazed. I might not have had as many friends as other girls, but that was because I was too busy reading books, making secret dens, daydreaming and talking with animals. The family dog had no choice but I was convinced that cats and squirrels listened to me, and then there were the birds.

Oh, the birds. I'd only known Katherine Mansfield as a prose writer when I came across her poem 'When I was a Bird', but it felt like meeting a soul mate. I don't know if it's a poem for children or adults, and I don't care. Its choppy form adds to its immediacy, and the mixture of long and short lines, the simplicity of language, and also the irresistible character of its fierce but naive narrator, are so perfectly judged. The girl in the poem (although it could be a boy) has an imagination as big as her heart, and the fact that both the daisies and 'Little Brother' don't believe her just makes the last line more delicious. I laugh at the daisies every time.

To me, the way we hear twice that her song doesn't have any words adds a layer of emotion to the words that *are* on the page. The title is also gorgeously definite. A poem called 'When I pretended to be a bird' would be much duller. Sometimes I worry if I'm over-identifying with the girl in the poem, but it's always comforting to read about other children who preferred collecting leaves to Barbies. And maybe it's a case study in how 'lonely losers' can grow up to be writers.

When I was a Bird

I climbed up the karaka tree
Into a nest all made of leaves
But soft as feathers.
I made up a song that went on singing all by itself
And hadn't any words, but got sad at the end.
There were daisies in the grass under the tree.
I said just to try them:
'I'll bite off your heads and give them to my little children to eat.'
But they didn't believe I was a bird;
They stayed quite open.
The sky was like a blue nest with white feathers
And the sun was the mother bird keeping it warm.
That's what my song said: though it hadn't any words.
Little Brother came up the path, wheeling his barrow.
I made my dress into wings and kept very quiet.
Then when he was quite near I said: 'Sweet, sweet!'
For a moment he looked quite startled;
Then he said: 'Pooh, you're not a bird; I can see your legs.'
But the daisies didn't really matter,
And Little Brother didn't really matter;
I felt just like a bird.

Katherine Mansfield

Vers De Société *by* Philip Larkin

The poem that's been a friend to Stephen Beresford

Being alone and being with other people – they're really the only two things that as a human you have to negotiate. That's what this poem wrestles with. Everybody knows that feeling of 'I don't want to go to your karaoke party', but Larkin takes you to the heart of why and what it means.

He opens with the invitation to the party that he doesn't want to go to. I know this dilemma, you think, I just need my space and quiet, and then I can write. But of course, it doesn't work like that. In the solitude the words don't come, and you sit there thinking about failure and remorse. So you put your coat on and you go to the party, frightening as it is, full of 'forks and faces', like a Bruegel painting. The protagonist changes; as a writer of drama that's of interest to me. The final shot is him arriving with some dreadful bottle of wine. There's humility in his arrival, shaking off his gabardine mac in the hall, pineapple and cheese on a stick, and off we go.

Larkin understands we have to be in the world and that the chatter is a way to distract ourselves from the ever-present knowledge of our own demise. In a way, that's something to celebrate. He's saying this is the experience of being alive, and you'd better face it. I often think about this: people know they're going to die and they still get up, go to Asda, buy the sausages and throw a barbecue. If that's not heroism, I don't know what is.

When I think about the purpose of art, it is to help us live, to help us walk through the world. This difficult, terrible, wonderful world. To hear something articulated brilliantly and perfectly settles you.

Vers De Société

My wife and I have asked a crowd of craps
To come and waste their time and ours: perhaps
You'd care to join us? In a pig's arse, friend.
Day comes to an end.
The gas fire breathes, the trees are darkly swayed.
And so *Dear Warlock-Williams: I'm afraid—*

Funny how hard it is to be alone.
I could spend half my evenings, if I wanted,
Holding a glass of washing sherry, canted
Over to catch the drivel of some bitch
Who's read nothing but *Which*;
Just think of all the spare time that has flown

Straight into nothingness by being filled
With forks and faces, rather than repaid
Under a lamp, hearing the noise of wind,
And looking out to see the moon thinned
To an air-sharpened blade.
A life, and yet how sternly it's instilled

All solitude is selfish. No one now
Believes the hermit with his gown and dish
Talking to God (who's gone too); the big wish
Is to have people nice to you, which means
Doing it back somehow.
Virtue is social. Are, then, these routines

Playing at goodness, like going to church?
Something that bores us, something we don't do well
(Asking that ass about his fool research)
But try to feel, because, however crudely,
It shows us what should be?
Too subtle, that. Too decent, too. Oh hell,

Only the young can be alone freely.
The time is shorter now for company,
And sitting by a lamp more often brings
Not peace, but other things.
Beyond the light stand failure and remorse
Whispering *Dear Warlock-Williams: Why, of course—*

Philip Larkin

Good Lord the Light *by* Christian Wiman

The poem that's been a friend to Krista Tippett

Christian Wiman is a wonderful poet. This is from his collection *Survival Is a Style*, written way before the pandemic. Reading this in 2020 put an end to any illusion we might have had that we know what will happen tomorrow, or even this hour. The poem still resonates with the questions we began asking then – what is real, what is true, what upholds us, what is essential? The careful, eloquent and beautiful language of this collection is a fitting container for the nobility of this struggle. The poet John O'Donohue once said to me, 'Beauty is not all loveliness,' and this poem is a beauty that is not all lovely.

Across time and cultures, when there is fracture, when words become weapons and when official and everyday language fails us, poetry emerges. I experienced this early in my life, in the 1980s in East Berlin. You'd be at a party, which might only be half legal, and you would wait for the poets to come. They were like rock stars, because they had this form for speaking truth. They were the heroes.

There's companionship on this page, even in those bleak opening lines, 'Good morning misery, / goodbye belief'. Those are hard things to say, to read, but they're true. They validate my experience and so even though there's a sadness and a weight to them, they help me settle into my fullest self. Putting words to the hardest things that happen, naming them, offers relief. The relief that we're telling the truth and we can work with the truth and we can walk with the truth.

When I'm being hard on myself for giving in to the difficulty of things, this is the friend that appears and says, you don't need to carry that extra burden of self-blame.

Good Lord the Light

Good morning misery,
goodbye belief,
good Lord the light
cutting across the lake
so long gone
to ice —

There is an under, always,
through which things still move, breathe,
and have their being,
quick coals and crimsons
no one need see
to see.

Good night knowledge,
goodbye beyond,
good God the winter
one must wander
one's own soul
to be.

Christian Wiman

You Don't Know What Love Is *by* Kim Addonizio

The poem that's been a friend to Salena Godden

Kim Addonizio's work here is fierce and spicy, it's boozy and punk, but it's also got substance, sensitivity and soul. It's fun and it's dangerous, like being too close to a fire. It will not be written off and will not be shushed.

I see my younger self in this poem. It's addressing the good old days and the bad choices, someone that brings out the worst in you, that brings chaos, destruction and sabotage.

At the same time she depicts aspects of love saving her – Love brings the dead girl up to the surface and is the tongue down the throat like an oxygen tube.

We all love a bit of danger; well, we think we do until we're dancing in our underwear and have no money, a terrible thirst, and we can't find our home. Looking for love in the wrong places, that resonates.

Those three words, 'So to hell', are so fascinating because they could mean two things. She could mean I won't have it, or she could mean why not? I'm drawn to the powerful ambiguity. Is she protecting herself? Or saying I can take it? There's a survival in there, a courage, which I salute and recognize.

When I was younger and wrote poems on these themes, I tended to be unkind to myself, or to paint myself as grotesque, but Kim is not doing that here. There's no guilt and there's no shame. That's what I admire and what I'm learning from this poem.

I like poetry to have a bit of spit and fire, to have a bit of fury and a bit of pepper on its tail. Kim really does that for me. This poem is the friend that would keep me up all night, help me drink all the tequilas, and sing with me until sunrise.

You Don't Know What Love Is

but you know how to raise it in me
like a dead girl winched up from a river. How to
wash off the sludge, the stench of our past.
How to start clean. This love even sits up
and blinks; amazed, she takes a few shaky steps.
Any day now she'll try to eat solid food. She'll want
to get into a fast car, one low to the ground, and drive
to some cinderblock shithole in the desert
where she can drink and get sick and then
dance in nothing but her underwear. You know
where she's headed, you know she'll wake up
with an ache she can't locate and no money
and a terrible thirst. So to hell
with your warm hands sliding inside my shirt
and your tongue down my throat
like an oxygen tube. Cover me
in black plastic. Let the mourners through.

Kim Addonizio

When Happiness returns after a long absence
by Penelope Shuttle

The poem that's been a friend to Victoria Field

This poem reminds me that small is beautiful; that things, especially recovery from loss, can take a long time; and that at the heart of the world is our domestic life. Written as an invocation, it takes nothing for granted and is both modest and magical. Here Happiness is a shapeshifter, wearing different costumes. Seeing our emotional life as a kind of drama appeals to me – all the world's a stage, as Shakespeare has it. It gives me a way to directly address, confront, speak to my feelings – Hello Happiness, go away Unhappiness!

I've always lived in an ensouled and creaturely world so I love the way this poem includes the small, busy companions who share our homes. We're not alone and we know now how vital insects are. The spider learning to spin her web again speaks to me of connection and quiet industry, and that resonates for me as a poet, aiming for a daily practice of writing.

Birds are more public, singing to the world. The merging of art and artifice with the beauty of a more-than-human existence is evoked by describing the wren as 'chanteuse of last light'. I find myself quoting that whenever I hear a blackbird singing on a rooftop, or a robin in a hedge.

This poem comes at the end of a collection with many poems about loss and grief, and it's been a friend to me ever since I first read it. It's also one I've shared with other people and it always strikes a chord: of hope, of possibility.

When Happiness returns after a long absence

When happiness returns, after a long absence,
she's a very small creature indeed,
an orderly marching ant,
scurrying beetle, or web-spinner

Let her be a spider,
learning to spin her web again,
lodging modestly behind the washer-dryer
in the back-kitchen,
earning her keep by waste disposal of flies

Let happiness be small, busy and eight-legged
for a couple of years —
Unhappiness, step out of my house,
go back to the wilderness,
where I can't hear the rustle of your black weeds
or even the shadow of your sobs

Now, raise your game, Happiness,
slip off your spider costume,
come to me in the shape of a wren
weaving your common or garden nest

I don't ask for an outbreak of joy so major
the police are called to quell it,
just your wren-song
drawing each no-longer-endless day to a close,
chanteuse of last light,
such modest happiness I think I can bear

Penelope Shuttle

Eve Remembering *by* Toni Morrison

The poem that's been a friend to Maria Augusta Arruda

I'm a pharmacologist, a geek who has spent most of her life inside a lab. I was the scientific one in a very artistic household. I had so many emotions that I didn't know how to manage. I found it easier to take on the pragmatic role, so poetry came later for me. It was a way of trying to understand better who I was.

Toni Morrison has always been a very strong figure for me, especially in how unapologetic she is about race. It can be difficult to find the words to talk about it clearly, to be surgical. So just like some people go to the Bible, or the Quran, I go to Toni.

I met this poem when I was recovering from a total hysterectomy, which brings with it a sense of a loss of womanhood. You go into the theatre a woman approaching middle age and come out an ancient woman. This poem found me in that moment and I started to see a beauty to this journey. When she says, 'Better the summit to see', it brings into perspective your life and your mortality, but without regrets.

The way the poem turns the story from the Bible around makes me think about my mum and grandma, what they went through as Black women in Brazil. They were betrayed by the expectation that being married would solve their problems, and when the myth of 'The Garden' collapsed, instead of living the lie they went into a kind of wilderness, into the adventure of uncertainty and risk. You harness the gale, you make it work for you.

When I look around at the hardships the human race is going through, I feel utterly bewildered. I don't dare to reach the summit, I don't think I'm going to get there, but the poem gives me hope.

Eve Remembering

1.

I tore from a limb fruit that had lost its green.
My hands were warmed by the heat of an apple
Fire red and humming.
I bit sweet power to the core.
How can I say what it was like?
The taste! The taste undid my eyes
And led me far from the gardens planted for a child
To wildernesses deeper than any master's call.

2.

Now these cool hands guide what they once caressed;
Lips forget what they have kissed.
My eyes now pool their light
Better the summit to see.

3.

I would do it all over again:
Be the harbor and set the sail,
Loose the breeze and harness the gale,
Cherish the harvest of what I have been.
Better the summit to scale.
Better the summit to be.

Toni Morrison

The Daughter *by* Carmen Giménez

The poem that's been a friend to Gita Ralleigh

I think of prose as a house you enter into, whereas poetry is something that goes into you, physically. I could really feel in my body the way this poem hit me.

As a writer, there's so much to admire here. There's a real freedom of form; the varying line length really allows the beauty of the phrase to take its time. Every thought is an image, a line unto itself. I absolutely love, 'Daughter, where did you get all that goddess?' I have a daughter and a son too; the fierceness of youth – that brightness, that fire – you don't ever want them to lose that.

There is this long line of a mother and a mother's mother, and you've all lived inside each other physically. She tugs on that rope and you can see the rope going forward and the rope going backwards.

This phrase, 'the gradual ebb of my mother's darkness', resonates with me as a feminist and in the context of being a woman from a minority, immigrant culture. In any immigrant childhood, there can be a darkness in your own history that's left behind. Then you have your own children and this new life opens up, new stories are written. Things are smoother for them than previous generations, but at the same time, you want them to have that grit that comes from an immigrant background.

I see a sort of intersection with my own experience as a writer and a doctor.

This ability to talk about the body, about motherhood, to reclaim this aspect of our experience in a way that for centuries women didn't really do in poetry, it resonates on so many levels. It felt like she was turning around and pointing at me going, 'Hey, listen to this.' It was arresting.

The Daughter

We said she was a negative image of me because of
    her lightness.
She's light and also passage, the glory in my cortex.
Daughter, where did you get all that goddess?
Her eyes are Neruda's two dark pools at twilight.
Sometimes she's a stranger in my home because I hadn't
    imagined her.
Who will her daughter be?
She and I are the gradual ebb of my mother's darkness.
I unfurl the ribbon of her life, and it's a smooth long
    hallway, doors flung open.
Her surface is a deflection is why.
Harm on her, harm on us all.
Inside her, my grit and timbre, my reckless.

Carmen Giménez

Return *by* C. P. Cavafy *tr. Rae Dalven*

The poem that's been a friend to John Davis

I received this poem back in 1981 at the tender age of twenty. The encounter was intense. I'd returned from a long trip around Europe, I was back in rainy London, and a volume of poems came through the post with this one handwritten on a separate sheet of paper. In Greece I had met and fallen in love with the person who sent it to me. I almost wept when I read it. I experienced a rush of emotion and a longing to go back, to return as the poem says, and to be with them, which ultimately is what I did. I've been living in Greece for thirty-six years now, speaking Greek and being a translator and living with the person who was and still is very dear to me, my partner in life.

It is a love poem, romantic, sensual. The Greeks would say it's erotic. The word 'erotica' in Greek is specifically the love between lovers. It's full of the body – almost all of our sensory experience crammed into fifty-seven words. It evokes the passion of one's first experiences of love, but also has this yearning that comes from experience and age – Cavafy was forty-nine when he wrote it. When I read it now, it has a more melancholy tone because it's about the loss of desire. It's reaching out to youth, to intensity of feeling and emotion, and yearning for this to be revived.

As a poet, Cavafy has been a friend to me. I went through a phase when I found it harder to read poetry, and Cavafy helped me to keep faith in poetry that touches my heart. We can read poetry for many reasons but ultimately, we need it to stir us into feeling and thinking. Cavafy achieves this. What more could you want from a friend?

Return

Return often and take me,
beloved sensation, return and take me –
when the memory of the body awakens,
and old desire runs again through the blood;
when the lips and the skin remember,
and the hands feel as if they touch again.

Return often and take me at night,
when the lips and the skin remember . . .

C. P. Cavafy
tr. Rae Dalven

The Friend that

Comforts and

Helps Me to

Move Forward

Remember *by* Christina Rossetti

The poem that's been a friend to Georgina Chatfield

My wonderful grandma died suddenly when I was seventeen. She was one of a kind. Classy, dignified, funny, mischievous, kind, generous, thoughtful, up for anything. She said to me, 'I'd try anything once.'

I'd not experienced the death of a close family member or friend before, and it was all a rush of new, unwanted emotions. I wasn't sure what to do about them, how to talk to family and friends. It was very upsetting for my mum – understandably the focus was on her – and I suppose I felt a bit lost in it all.

On the dining table, there was a pile of cards waiting for my mum's attention, and I leafed through them with their sympathetic words and apologetic tones aimed at someone else. An extra piece of paper slipped out of one of the cards, with this poem printed neatly on it. I remember there being a simple, short message in the card itself, which seemed fitting as the poem did the talking.

The words and themes of the poem – hands holding, the future, grief, remembering and smiling – really did speak to me. Tucked into a card, unexpectedly revealing themselves, like a friend might, when you need them, turning up and saying just the right thing.

As a grown-up in age, if not in attitude, the poem now seems like it's not clever enough in some ways; its simplicity is too easy. When I re-read it though, those earlier feelings still resonate and the words still make a strong connection – they've not lost their potency or relevance – and so I do remember and smile. And I'd try anything once.

Remember

Remember me when I am gone away,
  Gone far away into the silent land;
  When you can no more hold me by the hand,
Nor I half turn to go yet turning stay.
Remember me when no more day by day
  You tell me of our future that you plann'd:
  Only remember me; you understand
It will be late to counsel then or pray.
Yet if you should forget me for a while
  And afterwards remember, do not grieve:
  For if the darkness and corruption leave
A vestige of the thoughts that once I had,
Better by far you should forget and smile
  Than that you should remember and be sad.

Christina Rossetti

The Way through the Woods *by* Rudyard Kipling

The poem that's been a friend to Linda Collins

This poem was in one of my late daughter's many books of poetry. Victoria died in 2014. She took her own life on the first day back at school. Well-meaning people want you to move on, but that's not possible because you're utterly changed. All you can do is find ways to adapt, and to honour your loved one.

I was living in Singapore and hopelessly floundering, so I sought my late daughter's help – 'Victoria, what did we use to do that was good together? How can I grow in some way?' I began googling options, and a night course on speech and drama came up. I found myself with this wonderful bunch of young Singaporeans of all backgrounds, full of energy. I was much older, but they accepted me into the fold.

We had to learn to recite a poem in front of an examiner. We were given a selection and my eyes went straight to this one. Kipling is problematic now, especially in Singapore; his jingoistic British Empire standpoint – there are gratuitous, offensive references in his work. However, this poem carries a sense of deep loss that reflected what I was feeling. To see that on the page, and then to learn to recite it, externalized my pain in a very healing way.

I stood up and looked at the relentless judge at the end of the room. It was intimidating. I thought about Victoria and how she wouldn't want her mum up there mumbling away. She wouldn't want to see me caving in, she'd want to see me going forward, so I took a deep breath. I was breathing in oxygen, but also the love of my fellow students and unquantifiable things. If that breath goes right down to your knees, it gives you fortitude to keep going, to carry on. And so there I was; I got through the woods.

The Way through the Woods

They shut the road through the woods
Seventy years ago.
Weather and rain have undone it again,
And now you would never know
There was once a road through the woods
Before they planted the trees.
It is underneath the coppice and heath,
And the thin anemones.
Only the keeper sees
That, where the ring-dove broods,
And the badgers roll at ease,
There was once a road through the woods.

Yet, if you enter the woods
Of a summer evening late,
When the night-air cools on the trout-ringed pools
Where the otter whistles his mate,
(They fear not men in the woods,
Because they see so few.)
You will hear the beat of a horse's feet,
And the swish of a skirt in the dew,
Steadily cantering through
The misty solitudes,
As though they perfectly knew
The old lost road through the woods.
But there is no road through the woods.

Rudyard Kipling

Out of God's Hat *by* Hafiz *tr. Daniel Ladinsky*

The poem that's been a friend to Mariah Wilde

This poem has a vitality, movement and adventure that whisks you away on a journey. At points it feels unsettling and dizzying, like a bird's-eye view that gives you vertigo, but then it comes down low and captures the minute details of life with gentle attentiveness. It is sumptuous, visceral, and captures life with all its senses.

He seems to say that yearning and pushing for something intangible elsewhere is futile when your life is already perfect when looked at differently. It's not a stance of apathy. It's a reflection on all that is possible when we accept our identity as people that are loved and are capable of loving. This is the antithesis of a shyness based on feelings of iniquity. This is the kind of love that makes you fearless.

I think many can relate to retreating from wonderful things for fear of the unknown. Yet there are some who leap into uncertainty, because they dance with this flow, not against it. This is the part of the poem that I still come back to. What limitations might I be placing on myself, and where is my own shyness? The poem begs us to consider what wonders might be on the other side of the unknown if we were to hold on to just one 'known', and that any step we take forward is a courageous one worthy of love.

It's a friend who is the life and soul of the party, yet is also the kind, quietly confident wallflower that truly sees you and knows just what to say at the right time.

Out of God's Hat

The stars got poured into the sky
Out of a Magician's hat last night,
And all of them have fallen into my hair.
Some have even tangled my eyelashes
Into luminous, playful knots.

Wayfarer,
You are welcome to cut a radiant tress
That lays upon my shoulders.
Wrap it around your trembling heart and body
That craves divine comfort and warmth.

I am like a pitcher of milk
In the hands of a mother who loves you.

All of my contents now
Have been churned into dancing suns and moons.

Lean your sweet neck and mouth
Out of that dark nest where you hide,
I will pour effulgence into your mind.

Come spring
You can find me rolling in fields
That are exploding in
Holy battles

Of scents, of sounds – everything is
A brilliant colored nova on a stem.

Forest animals hear me laughing
And surrender their deepest instincts and fears,

They come charging into meadows
To lick my hands and face,

This makes me so happy,
I become so happy

That my rising wink turns into a magic baton.
When my soft-eyed creatures see that wonderful signal
We all burst into singing

And make strange and primal beautiful sounds!

My only regret in this world then becomes:

That your shyness keeps you from placing
Your starving body against God

And seeing the Beloved become so pleased
With your courage

That His belly begins to rock and rock,
Then more planets get to leap
Onto the welcome mat of existence
All because
Of your precious love.

The Friend has turned my verse into sacred pollen.
When a breeze comes by

Falcons and butterflies
And playful gangs of young angels
Mounted on emerald spears

Take flight from me like a great sandstorm
That can blind you to all but the Truth!

Dear one,
Even if you have no net to catch Venus

My music
Will circle this earth for hundreds of years
And fall like resplendent debris,
Holy seed, onto a fertile woman.

For Hafiz
Wants to help you laugh at your every
Desire.

Hafiz
Wants you to know

Your life within God's arms,
Your dance within God's
Arms

Is already

Perfect!

Hafiz
tr. Daniel Ladinsky

Tall Nettles *by* Edward Thomas

The poem that's been a friend to Robbie Burton

Three weeks after my husband died I walked the Ship Canal towpath, barely lifting my eyes from its stones and ruts. It was October and cold but that hardly mattered; wintry weather was just another kind of numbness. Oblivious to road or boat traffic, I crossed the swing bridge to the village shops and was soon retracing my steps down to the towpath. A short distance ahead, something white fluttered on the handrail. It turned out to be a laminated card printed with Edward Thomas's 'Tall Nettles', part of a trail celebrating National Poetry Day 2007. Someone had thought carefully about its location. Behind it stood an old tin hut almost hidden by nettles.

Rusting metal, limestone stiles, wild hedgerows . . . the first stanza of 'Tall Nettles' took me straight back to childhood holidays in Wales and to many happy narrowboat holidays with my husband and our children. For a few minutes my step was lighter, and I followed the trail for a while before resuming my trudge back home.

Of the poems I saw displayed that day, 'Tall Nettles' stayed with me. What had struck me most was the vividness of the poem's images and the memories they invoked. Its sense of hope seemed to pass me by. Or maybe I ignored it. Or absorbed it – but only my footsteps acknowledged it. Whichever way it was, it helped.

Tall Nettles

Tall nettles cover up, as they have done
These many springs, the rusty harrow, the plough
Long worn out, and the roller made of stone:
Only the elm butt tops the nettles now.

This corner of the farmyard I like most:
As well as any bloom upon a flower
I like the dust on the nettles, never lost
Except to prove the sweetness of a shower.

Edward Thomas

Seachange *by* Kate Genevieve

The poem that's been a friend to Prasanna Puwanarajah

Kate is a poet and a researcher. She works in the field of neuroscience and VR, and she's a climate activist, intrigued by the regeneration of life and love.

Sometimes there's a collision between where you are in your life and the thing that you see or read, that just hits a kind of harmonic. Something taps you on the shoulder, arrives in your life and insists on its presence.

I came across this poem after a really rough six months, an intense period of work and the break-up of an important relationship. It speaks to the start of new things, new hope, new people, and the tidal patterns of all that. There are shades of darkness and the sea's edge, and then there is a gold-seamed landscape, and she sees all this as possibility, as generosity. She's making an extraordinary leap of faith, of hope, expressed through tangible things – mountains, planets, oceans.

That image, gold-seamed, it's like the Japanese repair technique of *kintsugi*, fixing the cracks with gold, cherishing the breaks. A break can be a thing that snares you, the past written onto us in some way, or could there be another possibility? Can we learn to move forward, walk on with it? I think this is a poem about that act, the choice to accept the generosity of others, to accept the newness of a moment or a person.

I find the language of science really beautiful, and by that I mean the quiet poetry of observation, the triangulation and testing of a question. Good science is about a really clarified question revealing a very simple potential truth. And when poems do that, there's something prophetic about them; you feel like you can't say no to them.

Seachange
For LP

Perhaps we are riding the moon's path
along the sea edge,
where things are less clear
and more alive?

My heart, as full as the sea,
follows the shoreline with certainty,
for here is a path drawn by desire –
a route touched by your darkness,
and mine.

Moon-struck.
Lit up by her generosity,
touched by the light of strangers,
together with the old smile of wrinkled mountains
and all the living beings multiplying.

Something special grows in the emptiness –
not innocence returned –
but wholeness,
gold-seamed.

this night

This Day

on which so many doors fall open

Let go!

The ocean ever rushes in to fill space revealed
with unforced irrepressible energy.

We can no more control a life's story
than we can command the animals,
or hold back the tides,
or ordain the fated meetings of the world.
The door only opens at the right time.

Instead, receive the gifts of sea-change:
take the moon-lit path along the shore
and meet what's fresh returning.
At one with desires of earth,
awake to everything that's growing.

The mountain smiles.
She knows
it's more than time alone
heals shattered pieces:
it is the gift of other beings.

For suffering dissolves
Into the fullness of night,
with the memory that the dark bright night
shines with love.

May all have eyes to see, ears to hear,

this night –

as full as the sea –

beyond sense and naming.

Kate Genevieve

'Hope' is the thing with feathers *by* Emily Dickinson

The poem that's been a friend to Lucy Heuschen

I discovered Emily Dickinson as a student. It was so different from anything I'd read, and her whole way of writing captivated me. Then, over the years, I lost touch with poetry. I was working in law, very long hours in the city, and was focused on just getting through the day-to-day grind. Then, when I was diagnosed with cancer, this poem came back to me.

You find out during treatment what works for you and what doesn't. I wanted to write a journal about what I was experiencing, but words deserted me. It was like being in a fog. For someone who was used to being able to express themselves, it was really hard. So this poem became important and precious to me. I could read it and feel like somebody got me.

It wasn't the kernel of hope itself, so much as the way that she describes the feeling of being hopeful. This idea that you're in completely foreign territory, and just trying to figure things out as you go. You 'sing the tune without the words' but that doesn't mean you give up hope. When I first discovered the poem, it was a simple kind of positivity I connected with. Now, in my forties, after all my experiences, I notice the struggle in it, the violence and the extremity and this little bird wobbling, trying to figure out how to survive the storm. It speaks to me in a very different way now.

I thank Emily Dickinson for staying with me all these years. For being by my side and letting me know it's OK to feel extreme things, to suffer, yet hope is there and it never goes away. It keeps singing.

'Hope' is the thing with feathers

'Hope' is the thing with feathers -
That perches in the soul -
And sings the tune without the words -
And never stops - at all -

And sweetest - in the Gale - is heard -
And sore must be the storm -
That could abash the little Bird
That kept so many warm -

I've heard it in the chillest land -
And on the strangest Sea -
Yet - never - in Extremity,
It asked a crumb - of me.

Emily Dickinson

Old Mary *by* Gwendolyn Brooks

The poem that's been a friend to Pete Stones

There's nothing more exhilarating than for somebody's words to suddenly evoke in you another way of thinking or being.

My daughter Ivy has a severe chromosome disorder. Her challenges include not being able to speak, eat or walk. The first three years were incredibly hard. I found solace in poetry. I created a poetry box for Ivy, and every time I come across a poem I connect with, I handwrite it and put it in the box. It feels strange to do this as there's a good chance Ivy will never be able to read these poems. This one means as much to me as I hope one day it will mean to her.

I first read it at a point when my partner and I were realizing that our lives as parents were never going to be what everybody else had, and that Ivy may never have her independence. The poem was melancholy to me. It carried this idea that some aspirations and activities were going to be lost. Since then I've come to terms with what the future might hold. I recently picked the poem out of the box and it resonated with me in a whole new way.

I came to see this as a poem about releasing yourself from expectation. I look at that phrase, 'My last defense / Is the present tense', and think about the times when I was down to my last shred of strength, but that's also the moment when you start to rebuild. You begin to exist in the present tense, revel in small moments, taking joy in the little things that she does. If I focus on those seven words, it no longer hurts, and there's a sense of peace in that.

Old Mary

My last defense
Is the present tense.

It little hurts me now to know
I shall not go

Cathedral-hunting in Spain
Nor cherrying in Michigan or Maine.

Gwendolyn Brooks

The Prelude *by* William Wordsworth

The poem that's been a friend to Charlotte Walker

As part of my MA, I made my way through Wordsworth's thirteen-book poem. Small bombs would continually go off in my head, and I'd have to look up from the page to let something enormous settle in. Short pauses just to stop my brain from getting too dizzy.

These lines from the poem's first book on childhood and school-time have stuck with me like no others. At the time I encountered them, I was also engaged in a programme of counselling for an eating disorder I had suffered with for many years. Reading Wordsworth was a crucial part of my therapy and helped me to navigate my way through the confusion of the process.

'There is a dark / Invisible workmanship' – I've thought about these words so many times. I love the recognition of the inherent darkness that is a part of all of our minds and lives. What is so striking is the way Wordsworth here also helps me to reframe that darkness into something skilled. This idea of 'workmanship' is wise and active, as if the shadowy parts of ourselves that we don't want to recognize are actually the spaces where integration and 'reconciliation' can occur.

'The calm existence that is mine when I / Am worthy of myself' feels like a bringing together of things. It helped me to understand that the darker sides of myself were not things to reject or feel shame about, but important parts of who I am and signposts towards who I want to be.

The Prelude

The mind of Man is fram'd even like the breath
And harmony of music. There is a dark
Invisible workmanship that reconciles
Discordant elements, and makes them move
In one society. Ah me! that all
The terrors, all the early miseries
Regrets, vexations, lassitudes, that all
The thoughts and feelings which have been infus'd
Into my mind, should ever have made up
The calm existence that is mine when I
Am worthy of myself! Praise to the end!
Thanks likewise for the means! But I believe
That Nature, oftentimes, when she would frame
A favor'd Being, from his earliest dawn
Of infancy doth open out the clouds,
As at the touch of lightning, seeking him
With gentlest visitation; not the less,
Though haply aiming at the self-same end,
Does it delight her sometimes to employ
Severer interventions, ministry
More palpable, and so she dealt with me.

William Wordsworth

Friendship *by* Carrie Williams Clifford

The poem that's been a friend to Delphine Gray

When I first read this, it was as if a poem I had been looking for all my life had found me. It's that brilliant formulation in the penultimate line, 'the soul-kiss': it caught my heart and made me gasp out loud.

Over time I've kept this poem with me in my memory pocket. It's the kind of poem that on the wrong day I might have passed over. It feels a little old-fashioned maybe, the rhythm and rhyme of it, but that day, when I was in the doldrums after some disappointing news, it put its understanding touch on my knee.

I think friendship is such a powerful force in so many people's lives and yet we can take it for granted or treat it lightly. The deeper waters of friendship are where I think I have done most of my growing in life. I have also experienced passion and romance in friendship in ways that make it equal, if not superior, to 'traditional' romance.

I didn't know the poet until I met this poem. On finding out more about her life as an activist and the founder of women's sections within the movement for racial equality, the last line carries even more poignancy and power.

It's interesting the way the poem is in long-shot in the first half and then moves into close-up on those beautiful final images. I've got a handful of friends I'm lucky enough to have had close to me over many years, but I've also recently struck up a friendship that has come from nowhere. It's thrilling and intoxicating to me that friendship can form so suddenly and unexpectedly and move very fast into the soul-kiss.

Friendship

Not by the dusty stretch of days
Slow-gathering to lengthening years
   We measure friendship's chain,
But by the understanding touch,
The smile, the soul-kiss, yea, the tears
   That ease the load of pain

Carrie Williams Clifford

The Friend
I Admire

Pessimism is for Lightweights *by* Salena Godden

The poem that's been a friend to Hannah Jane Walker

As poets, we sometimes have the great privilege of being in a room full of people listening to us for this little bit of time. As a writer I think, what am I going to use that privilege for?

I first experienced this poem at a gig, Salena delivering her words live to an audience. It had an immediate impact. Here it was, a poem, alive in a room full of people, igniting hope, inspiring change. There was this really different energy in the room that I hadn't felt for a long time. Everyone in the audience charged up, thinking yes, I agree, and what are we going to do about it?

I'm a natural pessimist, so this poem was a good challenge to me. A provocation to recognize that it's not that useful to be pessimistic. Optimism, if it translates into action, is vital right now. We need to be able to imagine ourselves out of some of the problems we've created and to see a different future.

The poem reminds us that everything incrementally adds up. It embodies what hope does, how it gathers through individuals and collectives. We might be up against what seem like insurmountable challenges, but this is about a belief that our individual choices aren't futile. It's a poem that says, we are all the people that we've been waiting for, the people who can solve the problem.

This poem, it's got some fight in it. It's a friend that challenges me.

Pessimism is for Lightweights

Think of those that marched this road before
And those that will march here in years to come
The road in shadow and the road in the sun
The road before us and the road all done
History is watching us and what will we become

This road is all flags and milestones
Immigrant blood and sweat and tears
Built this city, built this country
Made this road last all these years

This road is made of protest
And those not permitted to vote
And those that are still fighting to speak
With a boot stamping on their throat

There is power and strength in optimism
To have faith and to stay true to you
Because if you can look in the mirror
And have belief and promise you
Will share wonder in living things
Beauty, dreams, books and art
Love your neighbour and be kind
And have an open heart

Then you're already winning at living
You speak up, you show up and stand tall
It's silence that is complicit
It's apathy that hurts us all

Pessimism is for lightweights
There is no straight white line
It's the bumps and curves and obstacles
That make this road yours and mine

Pessimism is for lightweights
This road was never easy and straight
And living is all about living alive and lively
And love will conquer hate

Salena Godden

The Death by Heroin of Sid Vicious *by* Paul Durcan

The poem that's been a friend to John Crowley

What first struck me about this poem was how it pulls together two familiar sets of imagery into a context that doesn't make any sense, and somehow blasts a light on the human condition in the middle of it all.

Paul Durcan was the first poet whose work I owned. I also remember buying a copy of *Never Mind the Bollocks* by the Sex Pistols around the same time in 1985; long after it had come out, but that cover artwork and the sound of what lay inside had lost none of its potency. It felt like a dangerous, slightly incendiary thing to put on the record player. The album's power has waned for me over the years, but the poem's has grown. There is the language of Second World War escape movies, the well-worn tropes of watchtowers, searchlights, going over the wire. It struck me as a brilliant fusing of ostensibly unrelated images. It's a major poem in which he unpacks two different kinds of nihilism: a grand-scale historical nihilism of death camps, and as it were a lighter kind of nihilism, the pop culture nihilism of punk.

Nothing about this poem is anything less than completely surprising to me – including its wit. It affects me every time I read it, and like any good piece of writing it is endlessly open to interpretation.

There's an open compassion in Durcan's work. It's almost like he's got fewer layers of skin than others. He's very easily moved but not in a sentimental way. He's affected by the world and seeks imagery that can meet that level of feeling.

The Death by Heroin of Sid Vicious

There – but for the clutch of luck – go I.

At daybreak – in the arctic fog of a February daybreak –
Shoulder-length helmets in the watchtowers of the
      concentration camp
Caught me out in the intersecting arcs of the swirling
      searchlights.

There were at least a zillion of us caught out there –
Like ladybirds under a boulder –
But under the microscope each of us was unique,

Unique and we broke for cover, crazily breasting
The barbed wire and some of us made it
To the forest edge, but many of us did not

Make it, although their unborn children did –
Such as you whom the camp commandant branded
Sid Vicious of the Sex Pistols. Jesus, break his fall:

There – but for the clutch of luck – go we all.

Paul Durcan

A Recovered Memory of Water *by* Nuala Ní Dhomhnaill
tr. Paul Muldoon

The poem that's been a friend to Pádraig Ó Tuama

Nuala Ní Dhomhnaill's image was on the front cover of the Irish language poetry book we used at school, and one day she came into our class to read. She was magnificent. I was transfixed. As she spoke in gorgeous Irish, I witnessed in her, not only the recital of a poem, but the being of a poem.

Here she expresses, in the most extraordinary way, the experience of Irish people whose language – a language that had been spoken for hundreds and hundreds of years – was being very quickly removed. In the poem, mermaids have come to land and while their children have a memory of water in them on a DNA level, it's not a conscious one. She's evoking a state of where, even if you don't know a language, something in your body remembers, and you're made strange by it. What does it mean to remember things that you have never experienced but that nonetheless are in your bones?

Tír gan teanga, tír gan anam: a land without a language is a land without a soul. One method of colonization is to remove people's indigenous fluency in their own language so they have to learn a foreign language to negotiate for their safety.

I think language and poetry is a type of prayer and an answer to that prayer. I'm not speaking about prayer in a theological sense; I'm speaking about prayer as a deep yearning. I'm in debt to Nuala Ní Dhomhnaill and her poem for its truth telling, for not shying away from the complicated conversations about the legacy of language, and the lament for a language that's been removed through a process of colonization. I love the possibility this poem presents by employing a register of sadness, rather than a register of hatred.

A Recovered Memory of Water

Sometimes when the mermaid's daughter
is in the bathroom
cleaning her teeth with a thick brush
and baking soda
she has the sense the room is filling
with water.

It starts at her feet and ankles
and slides further and further up
over her thighs and hips and waist.
In no time
it's up to her oxters.
She bends down into it to pick up
handtowels and washcloths and all such things
as are sodden with it.
They all look like seaweed—
like those long strands of kelp that used to be called
'mermaid-hair' or 'foxtail.'
Just as suddenly the water recedes
and in no time
the room's completely dry again.

A terrible sense of stress
is part and parcel of these emotions.
At the end of the day she has nothing else
to compare it to.
She doesn't have the vocabulary for any of it.
At her weekly therapy session
she has more than enough to be going on with
just to describe this strange phenomenon
and to express it properly
to the psychiatrist.

She doesn't have the terminology
or any of the points of reference
or any word at all that would give the slightest suggestion
as to what water might be.
'A transparent liquid,' she says, doing as best she can.
'Right,' says the therapist, 'keep going.'
He coaxes and cajoles her towards word-making.
She has another run at it.
'A thin flow,' she calls it,
casting about gingerly in the midst of the words.
'A shiny film. Dripping stuff. Something wet.'

Nuala Ní Dhomhnaill
tr. Paul Muldoon

Love Song for Words *by* Nazik al-Mala'ika
tr. Rebecca C. Johnson

The poem that's been a friend to Maryam Alsaeid

My parents are Iraqi and this was my introduction to Iraqi poetry – it blew me away. Nazik al-Mala'ika was the first Arabic poet to use free verse, a pioneer. She let go of any fear of people's perception of the form. For her, it was always about being authentic, and she was very passionate about women's rights and being able to use her voice. This poem feels like she's telling herself to speak those words that are rich and beautiful and that she wants to send out into the world.

This poem is not saying that words are always pure and elegant, or that they're going to save you, be your heroes. It's saying sometimes words are dreamy, wonderful, but they can also be very painful. She creates an alchemy that makes hurtful experiences become beautiful. This infuses me with a new zest for writing and poetry and gives me my voice again.

'Why do we fear words' – I can't help but relate to that. I've always been told to suppress how I feel in certain parts of my life – 'that's too much, that's too intense, don't share that' – but perhaps being vulnerable and allowing myself to be in those states of intensity is the most courageous thing I can do. Giving myself permission to feel and then to write in whatever style arrives, that's the bravest thing I can do.

There can be a Catch-22; you can see that with social media, you want to be seen but you're afraid of how you will come across. Ultimately it's just so much more important to live authentically. When you're authentic, you leave behind a fragrance, you lay a path for other people to be authentic too.

Love Song for Words

Why do we fear words
when they have been rose-palmed hands,
fragrant, passing gently over our cheeks,
and glasses of heartening wine
sipped, one summer, by thirsty lips?

Why do we fear words
when among them are words like unseen bells,
whose echo announces in our troubled lives
the coming of a period of enchanted dawn,
drenched in love, and life?
So why do we fear words?

We took pleasure in silence.
We became still, fearing the secret might part our lips.
We thought that in words laid an unseen ghoul,
crouching, hidden by the letters from the ear of time.
We shackled the thirsty letters,
we forbade them to spread the night for us
as a cushion, dripping with music, dreams,
and warm cups.

Why do we fear words?
Among them are words of smooth sweetness
whose letters have drawn the warmth of hope from two lips,
and others that, rejoicing in pleasure
have waded through momentary joy with two drunk eyes.
Words, poetry, tenderly
turned to caress our cheeks, sounds
that, asleep in their echo, lies a rich color, a rustling,
a secret ardor, a hidden longing.

Why do we fear words?
If their thorns have once wounded us,
then they have also wrapped their arms around our necks
and shed their sweet scent upon our desires.
If their letters have pierced us
and their face turned callously from us
Then they have also left us with an oud in our hands
And tomorrow they will shower us with life.
So pour us two full glasses of words!

Tomorrow we will build ourselves a dream-nest of words,
high, with ivy trailing from its letters.
We will nourish its buds with poetry
and water its flowers with words.
We will build a balcony for the timid rose
with pillars made of words,
and a cool hall flooded with deep shade,
guarded by words.

Our life we have dedicated as a prayer
To whom will we pray . . . but to words?

Nazik al-Mala'ika
tr. Rebecca C. Johnson

The Love Song of J. Alfred Prufrock *by* T. S. Eliot

The poem that's been a friend to Ella Frears

This was one of the first poems that we studied at university. I was struck by how connected I felt to this strange, uptight man in his twenties, from around the 1920s. I can see myself back then waking up after a heavy night out and thinking, *I should have been a pair of ragged claws scuttling across the floors of silent seas.* I still feel that connection – I know that interior voice, that weary, lonesome voice.

There's this feeling of the inexpressible. Prufrock's voice lacks confidence. He's constantly frustrated by his inability to act. We don't know what the overwhelming question is that he keeps driving at. For me, there's a romantic frustration behind it, but also something more existential: 'I have seen the moment of my greatness flicker, / And I have seen the eternal Footman hold my coat, and snicker'.

There is a lack of confidence in the speaker, but also the complete confidence of the poet. It takes a lot to end a poem without resolving the whole conceit that you've built. Poetry is my favourite of the written forms, the way that it uses music, shape and space. It can be incantatory or conversational, intimate and cinematic. Eliot constantly surprises us with the pace of the stanzas, with the rhythm of them, with the way that they move and what's happening. I find that so exciting.

Eliot's ability to be self-aware and self-deprecating within a poem, to refuse the reader things – answers, for example, but also not to shut them out. To do all this and to do it with style.

It's that sweet, nerdy friend who might get worked up about a particular thing at a party and then feel very embarrassed after. He's always been in love with you, but he's never said.

The Love Song of J. Alfred Prufrock

S'io credesse che mia risposta fosse
A persona che mai tornasse al mondo,
Questa fiamma staria senza piu scosse.
Ma percioche giammai di questo fondo
Non torno vivo alcun, s'i'odo il vero,
Senza tema d'infamia ti rispondo.

Let us go then, you and I,
When the evening is spread out against the sky
Like a patient etherized upon a table;
Let us go, through certain half-deserted streets,
The muttering retreats
Of restless nights in one-night cheap hotels
And sawdust restaurants with oyster-shells:
Streets that follow like a tedious argument
Of insidious intent
To lead you to an overwhelming question . . .
Oh, do not ask, "What is it?"
Let us go and make our visit.

In the room the women come and go
Talking of Michelangelo.

The yellow fog that rubs its back upon the window-panes,
The yellow smoke that rubs its muzzle on the window-panes,
Licked its tongue into the corners of the evening,
Lingered upon the pools that stand in drains,
Let fall upon its back the soot that falls from chimneys,
Slipped by the terrace, made a sudden leap,
And seeing that it was a soft October night,
Curled once about the house, and fell asleep.

And indeed there will be time
For the yellow smoke that slides along the street,
Rubbing its back upon the window-panes;
There will be time, there will be time
To prepare a face to meet the faces that you meet;
There will be time to murder and create,
And time for all the works and days of hands
That lift and drop a question on your plate;
Time for you and time for me,
And time yet for a hundred indecisions,
And for a hundred visions and revisions,
Before the taking of a toast and tea.

In the room the women come and go
Talking of Michelangelo.

And indeed there will be time
To wonder, 'Do I dare?' and, 'Do I dare?'
Time to turn back and descend the stair,
With a bald spot in the middle of my hair —
(They will say: "How his hair is growing thin!")
My morning coat, my collar mounting firmly to the chin,
My necktie rich and modest, but asserted by a simple pin —
(They will say: "But how his arms and legs are thin!")
Do I dare
Disturb the universe?
In a minute there is time
For decisions and revisions which a minute will reverse.

For I have known them all already, known them all:
Have known the evenings, mornings, afternoons,
I have measured out my life with coffee spoons;
I know the voices dying with a dying fall
Beneath the music from a farther room.
    So how should I presume?

And I have known the eyes already, known them all—
The eyes that fix you in a formulated phrase,
And when I am formulated, sprawling on a pin,
When I am pinned and wriggling on the wall,
Then how should I begin
To spit out all the butt-ends of my days and ways?
    And how should I presume?

And I have known the arms already, known them all—
Arms that are braceleted and white and bare
(But in the lamplight, downed with light brown hair!)
Is it perfume from a dress
That makes me so digress?
Arms that lie along a table, or wrap about a shawl.
    And should I then presume?
    And how should I begin?

Shall I say, I have gone at dusk through narrow streets
And watched the smoke that rises from the pipes
Of lonely men in shirt-sleeves, leaning out of windows? . . .

I should have been a pair of ragged claws
Scuttling across the floors of silent seas.

And the afternoon, the evening, sleeps so peacefully!
Smoothed by long fingers,
Asleep . . . tired . . . or it malingers,
Stretched on the floor, here beside you and me.
Should I, after tea and cakes and ices,
Have the strength to force the moment to its crisis?
But though I have wept and fasted, wept and prayed,
Though I have seen my head (grown slightly bald) brought in
        upon a platter,
I am no prophet — and here's no great matter;
I have seen the moment of my greatness flicker,
And I have seen the eternal Footman hold my coat, and snicker,
And in short, I was afraid.

And would it have been worth it, after all,
After the cups, the marmalade, the tea,
Among the porcelain, among some talk of you and me,
Would it have been worth while,
To have bitten off the matter with a smile,
To have squeezed the universe into a ball
To roll it towards some overwhelming question,
To say: "I am Lazarus, come from the dead,
Come back to tell you all, I shall tell you all"—
If one, settling a pillow by her head
   Should say: That is not what I meant at all;
   That is not it, at all."

And would it have been worth it, after all,
Would it have been worth while,
After the sunsets and the dooryards and the sprinkled streets,
After the novels, after the teacups, after the skirts that trail
      along the floor—
And this, and so much more?—
It is impossible to say just what I mean!
But as if a magic lantern threw the nerves in patterns on
      a screen:
Would it have been worth while
If one, settling a pillow or throwing off a shawl,
And turning toward the window, should say:
   "That is not it at all,
   That is not what I meant, at all."

No! I am not Prince Hamlet, nor was meant to be;
Am an attendant lord, one that will do
To swell a progress, start a scene or two,
Advise the prince; no doubt, an easy tool,
Deferential, glad to be of use,
Politic, cautious, and meticulous;
Full of high sentence, but a bit obtuse;

At times, indeed, almost ridiculous—
Almost, at times, the Fool.

I grow old . . . I grow old . . .
I shall wear the bottoms of my trousers rolled.

Shall I part my hair behind? Do I dare to eat a peach?
I shall wear white flannel trousers, and walk upon the beach.
I have heard the mermaids singing, each to each.

I do not think that they will sing to me.

I have seen them riding seaward on the waves
Combing the white hair of the waves blown back
When the wind blows the water white and black.
We have lingered in the chambers of the sea
By sea-girls wreathed with seaweed red and brown
Till human voices wake us, and we drown.

T. S. Eliot

The Young Taoist Transcends His Body *by* Linda Chase

The poem that's been a friend to Martin Kratz

Linda was my first poetry teacher. She sent me this poem in response to something I had submitted but was unsure of. Having a poet and teacher who you respect saying, 'Oh, your poem made me think of something of mine,' was significant for me. It gave me permission to write in this expansive way; I didn't just have to write observational poems about real things like gardens, it was OK to write a poem about flying to the moon.

I remember being struck by the easy confidence in the tone of the poem, how it enters the world with this simple 'Let me tell you'. This confident, conversational voice reminds me of O'Hara. There's a certain kind of freedom, an uninhibited straight talking.

The poem is about both the things that can hold you back and the idea of transcendence. It's unusual for that to incorporate rage, but here it does. It's almost a nuclear thing that the young Taoist's body releases, huge energy that could own all the sky. The things that could stop him, they're everywhere – coming down the walls, the cracks appearing gradually, it's one thing after another until they're destroyed and the body itself has become this firework that explodes. The poem leaves you at the point of transcendence. Writing can be like that, intense effort and then release. It's only very brief, this moment of freedom.

Linda died a few years after she gave me the poem, and one of her friends read it at her memorial service. Over the years it's continued to come back to me as one of a number of poems that liberate me as a writer. There are other poems I could choose, but this is the one that's written into the foundation of what I do.

The Young Taoist Transcends His Body

In less than two hours,
he managed to move his whole body
through his hands,
as the centres of his palms opened.
His eyes widened,
the pupils spread out into blue irises
and his mind released
like the top of a baby's head.
The walls, covered in murals,
turned to paper as the night sky
slid in through the cracks
and his own thoughts slipped out,
shaped like Chinese kites,
self-igniting, tails of fire, soaring
in competition with the moon.

Let me tell you, the moon
was not a sliver that night.
It was one day off being full
and he chased it shamelessly.
A paper dragon, flames lashing
his own body from behind,
he raged, red-orange across the sky
with ground glass glued
to his reeled out string.
He could have cut the moon to shreds
since all the sky belonged to him
and all the fire was his plaything.
What a famous rush of wind he made,
what a stirring. I tell you,
it was a glorious way to go out.

Linda Chase

O Captain! My Captain! *by* Walt Whitman

The poem that's been a friend to Farah Karim-Cooper

The year I graduated from high school, I went to see the film *Dead Poets Society*, came home and said, 'Dad, I'm gonna be an English teacher.' That film opened up a whole world for me. The poem comes at the end, when the boys recognize how much their teacher has done for them. For this one moment in their lives they were meeting their souls, and that's what happened for me that summer too. Here I am thirty years later: I have a PhD in English, I teach poetry, and I work at Shakespeare's Globe.

As a fellow American, Walt Whitman is important to me because he's a poet of democracy. The poem was written for Abraham Lincoln when he was assassinated, and the metaphor of the ship and the journey is the Civil War. Whitman called Lincoln the Redeemer president. He represents the high hope that Americans have for that office. As a child of an immigrant, and someone who was introduced to the American Dream as a gift, reading Walt Whitman in the light of what's happened in the last decade, it's like a heartbreak. The poem has become a lament for the loss of leadership that upholds those ideals of American democracy.

The first time I heard this poem, I thought about my dad, who is a retired sea captain. He's incredibly soulful and the sea is inside him. He's also a poet, he writes prolifically. A lot of the person that I am today was formed by watching him and listening to him.

This poem is like a friend I didn't know I had. Someone who tapped me on the shoulder one day and said, 'I don't think you're making the right choice here.' At that important moment in my young adult life, Whitman, or certainly this poem, was that friend.

O Captain! My Captain!

O Captain! my Captain! our fearful trip is done,
The ship has weather'd every rack, the prize we sought is won,
The port is near, the bells I hear, the people all exulting,
While follow eyes the steady keel, the vessel grim and daring;
        But O heart! heart! heart!
          O the bleeding drops of red,
            Where on the deck my Captain lies,
            Fallen cold and dead.

O Captain! my Captain! rise up and hear the bells;
Rise up—for you the flag is flung—for you the bugle trills,
For you bouquets and ribbon'd wreaths—for you the shores
    a-crowding,
For you they call, the swaying mass, their eager faces turning;
        Here Captain! dear father!
          This arm beneath your head!
           It is some dream that on the deck,
            You've fallen cold and dead.

My Captain does not answer, his lips are pale and still,
My father does not feel my arm, he has no pulse nor will,
The ship is anchor'd safe and sound, its voyage closed and done,
From fearful trip the victor ship comes in with object won;
        Exult O shores, and ring O bells!
          But I with mournful tread,
           Walk the deck my Captain lies,
           Fallen cold and dead.

Walt Whitman

Pyramid Scheme *by* Hera Lindsay Bird

The poem that's been a friend to Rupert Goold

I really admire this poet; she wasn't even thirty when she wrote this poem that gives words to thoughts that I can't even begin to express. She has a turn of phrase that pivots from the everyday to the sublime in a completely organic way. I'm really drawn to those works of art that capture a momentary bliss, and this is as fresh as spring dew on city railings. Maybe it's because she's from a part of the world less burdened by literary heritage, but it feels like she's able to unfurl her verses as effortlessly as a sail.

As a director I often feel the challenge of trying to resolve my pragmatic, rational, analytical side with my more playful, intuitive, creative one. I enjoy the echoes of that here. She attempts to describe how two indescribable things work – a complex and seemingly non-sensical financial scheme, and love. Her feelings about love and her relationship to this person are counterpointed against capitalism. We usually think of trickle-down economics as a negative thing but here, when she says 'or was love the real pyramid scheme?', there's a sense that if you pass love down, it does come back to you.

I love 'i don't know where this poem ends'. It's a sort of game; she's saying, I don't really know what this metaphor is about, I'm just feeling my way towards something that is like life, and like love. But of course, she's aware of the artifice she's creating. It feels like reading the unedited first draft of something, even though you know she has incredible technical ability and she's probably spent weeks doing it.

It would be the friend that isn't afraid to seriously mock me and puncture any pretensions I have, but from a place of safety and affection.

Pyramid Scheme

the other day i was thinking about the term pyramid scheme,
      and why they called it pyramid scheme and not
      triangle scheme
and i asked you what you thought
you thought it added a certain gravitas, and linked the idea of
      economic prosperity
with some of history's greatest architectural achievements
unconsciously suggesting a silent wealth of gold and heat
a triangle is two dimensional, and therefore
a less striking mental image than the idea of a third dimension
      of financial fraud
which is how many dimensions of financial fraud the term
      pyramid scheme suggests
but i had to pause for a second at the financial fraud part
because it occurred to me i didn't know what pyramid schemes
      really were
i knew they had something to do with people getting money
      from nothing
like
the person at the top of the pyramid scheme, or more accurately
triangle scheme, acquires a number of investors and takes
      their money
and then pays the first lot of investors with the money from
      another bunch of investors
and so on and so forth
all the way to the bottom of the triangle
or pyramid face
which is the kind of stupid thing that happens
if you keep your money in a pyramid and not a bank account
although if you ask me banks are the real pyramid schemes
      after all
or was love the real pyramid scheme? i can't remember

maybe it's better to keep your money in a pyramid than
        a bank
and i should shop around and compare the interest rates
        on different pyramids
maybe i should open up a savings pyramid
with a whole bunch of trapdoors and malarias
to keep the financial anthropologists
i mean bankers out
my emeralds cooling under the ground like beautiful
        women's eyes

i think this was supposed to be a metaphor for something
but i can't remember where i was going with it
and now it's been swept away by the winds of
whatever
but knowing me, it was probably love
that great dark blue sex hope that keeps coming true
that cartoon black castle with a single bird flying over it

i don't know where this poem ends
how far below the sand
but it's still early evening
and you and I are a little drunk
you answer the phone
you pour me a drink
i know you hate the domestic in poetry but you should
        have thought of that before you invited me to
        move in with you
i used to think arguments were the same as honesty
i used to think screaming was the same as passion
i used to think pain was meaningful
i no longer think pain is meaningful
i never learned anything good from being unhappy
i never learned anything good from being happy either
the way i feel about you has nothing to do with learning

it has nothing to do with anything
but i feel it down in the corners of my sarcophagus
i feel it in my sleep
even when i am not thinking about you
you are still pouring through my blood, like fire through
      an abandoned hospital ward
these coins are getting heavy on my eyes
it has been a great honor and privilege to love you
it has been a great honor and privilege to eat cold pizza
      on your steps at dawn
love is so stupid: it's like punching the sun
and having a million gold coins rain down on you
which you don't even have to pay tax on
because sun money is free money
and i'm pretty sure there are no laws about that
but i would pay tax
because i believe that hospitals and education
and the arts should be publicly funded
even this poem
when i look at you, my eyes are two identical
      neighborhood houses on fire
when i look at you my eyes bulge out of my skull like a
      dog in a cartoon
when i am with you
an enormous silence descends upon me
and i feel like i am sinking into the deepest part of my life
we walk down the street, with the grass blowing back
      and forth
i have never been so happy

Hera Lindsay Bird

Kubla Khan *by* Samuel Taylor Coleridge

The poem that's been a friend to Gregory Leadbetter

I can trace the fact of my being a poet back to this poem. It taught me that the lyric can be mythic, and the mythic can be lyric. When I was seventeen, its ecstatic quality hit me straight away and created a sort of synaptic flood across my brain. For a long time I couldn't explain what was so arresting, enlivening and animating about it. It's intensely musical. There is this very strong, regular, metrical pattern, combined with extraordinary imagery that is diffused and modulated across that rhythm. You can't paraphrase what's going on – it's doing something that works by the power of its own image in ways that defy easy explanation.

It also appealed to me because it was about origination, creation, the source of things. Coleridge is playing on the source of life and the source of language – this intimate connection between physical, organic life and language. Language is a form of touch and itself a source of life. That awakening energy that I felt when I read it altered me. It woke something up in me.

Our experiences can become conditioned by the poetry we read. Poetry can get into 'the blood and vital juices of our minds', in Wordsworth's wonderful phrase. It can switch on senses that we might not otherwise have had in our interactions with the world. Poetry of this order gets into the very fabric of your thinking.

'Kubla Khan' is a friend at once intimate and distanced – extremely charismatic, but at the same time generous and not at all egotistical. There's something profoundly giving in what this poem does. It is a gift.

Kubla Khan

Or, a vision in a dream. A Fragment.

In Xanadu did Kubla Khan
A stately pleasure-dome decree:
Where Alph, the sacred river, ran
Through caverns measureless to man
   Down to a sunless sea.
So twice five miles of fertile ground
With walls and towers were girdled round;
And there were gardens bright with sinuous rills,
Where blossomed many an incense-bearing tree;
And here were forests ancient as the hills,
Enfolding sunny spots of greenery.

But oh! That deep romantic chasm which slanted
Down the green hill athwart a cedarn cover!
A savage place! As holy and enchanted
As e'er beneath a waning moon was haunted
By woman wailing for her demon-lover!
And from this chasm, with ceaseless turmoil seething,
As if this earth in fast thick pants were breathing,
A mighty fountain momently was forced:
Amid whose swift half-intermitted burst
Huge fragments vaulted like rebounding hail,
Or chaffy grain beneath the thresher's flail:
And mid these dancing rocks at once and ever
It flung up momently the sacred river.
Five miles meandering with a mazy motion
Through wood and dale the sacred river ran,
Then reached the caverns measureless to man,
And sank in tumult to a lifeless ocean;
And 'mid this tumult Kubla heard from far
Ancestral voices prophesying war!

The shadow of the dome of pleasure
Floated midway on the waves;
Where was heard the mingled measure
From the fountain and the caves.
It was a miracle of rare device,
A sunny pleasure-dome with caves of ice!

A damsel with a dulcimer
In a vision once I saw:
It was an Abyssinian maid
And on her dulcimer she played,
Singing of Mount Abora.
Could I revive within me
Her symphony and song,
To such a deep delight 'twould win me,
That with music loud and long,
I would build that dome in air,
That sunny dome! Those caves of ice!
And all who heard should see them there,
And all should cry, Beware! Beware!
His flashing eyes, his floating hair!
Weave a circle round him thrice,
And close your eyes with holy dread
For he on honey-dew hath fed,
And drunk the milk of Paradise.

Samuel Taylor Coleridge

I Am! *by* John Clare

The poem that's been a friend to Brian Cox

For me, the late eighteenth into the nineteenth century is one of the most exciting times in poetry because it started to become free and to find a new urgency of expression and opinion.

John Clare was a peasant, a farmer poet from Northamptonshire. He had so little, survived extreme hardship and made this amazing work. In his fifties, he writes this poem 'I Am!' When I first read it, I couldn't quite believe it had been written in 1844, because the modernity of it is so overwhelming. The man just goes straight to the point.

It's about crisis; how after a life of struggle, a man is forced to deal with the self in the most fundamental way. He is coming to the core of who he is, and it is very painful and so he writes this poem. It's a triumph of craft. It's astonishing that he was able to write such a goal-scoring poem.

He's not a classicist in any way; his vocabulary would have been very narrow and he would have had to develop it himself. Coming from a certain background, I had to do the same. I didn't study the classics; there was no access to them. I was very lucky to be a student in the sixties. I was welcomed and encouraged – that's what social mobility did. At drama school we did an hour on poetry every week, and it was a fantastic way of really understanding language and the value of it. Working on Shakespeare, you discover that word and rhythm and sense are very much interlinked; you really get the visceral power of poetry.

I think a poem like 'I Am!' simply says, the human condition is very fragile – don't forget it, and you need a pal to remind you of that.

As for the poem that's been a friend to Logan Roy? It would probably be 'This Be The Verse' by Philip Larkin: 'They fuck you up, your mum and dad.' Yes, I think that's a sentiment he would completely understand.

I Am!

I am—yet what I am none cares or knows;
My friends forsake me like a memory lost:
I am the self-consumer of my woes—
They rise and vanish in oblivious host,
Like shadows in love's frenzied stifled throes
And yet I am, and live—like vapours tossed

Into the nothingness of scorn and noise,
Into the living sea of waking dreams,
Where there is neither sense of life or joys,
But the vast shipwreck of my life's esteems;
Even the dearest that I loved the best
Are strange—nay, rather, stranger than the rest.

I long for scenes where man hath never trod
A place where woman never smiled or wept
There to abide with my Creator, God,
And sleep as I in childhood sweetly slept,
Untroubling and untroubled where I lie
The grass below—above the vaulted sky.

John Clare

Fern Hill *by* Dylan Thomas

The poem that's been a friend to Adrian Tissier

I first encountered this poem when I was leaving home, going to Sheffield University. My brother took me to St Pancras and, as he was helping me onto the train with my cases, he put a copy of *The Penguin Book of English Verse* in my hand. 'Look at the last poem, I think you'll like it,' he said. So as I began my journey, with a real mix of emotions, there it was, 'Fern Hill'.

It was comforting and thought provoking. Dylan Thomas celebrates the innocence and freedom of childhood, while lamenting its inevitable loss. I love the tumbling combination of images, the rich creativity of the language. It has a really sensuous quality to it. He's combining past and present, young and old, living and dying. The juxtaposition of ideas and images is really impressive. There's a looseness and a freeness with his thinking and his ability to piece things together. I'm in awe of his use of repetition, the way he returns to ideas, colours and words, but in a way that's fresh and that sings.

This poem works on the head, the heart and the soul. I'm drawn to intuitive ways of being rather than analytical and I really respond to the playfulness here. It feels effortless, almost as if it's written itself, and yet it is clearly so carefully crafted. The joy of the poem outweighs the melancholy. It's a poem that reaffirms life. Most of all, it's a celebration of us, childhood and our connection with nature.

The words in this poem are just as powerful now as when I read them on that train. It's amazing that my brother just knew there was a poem so right for that moment.

Fern Hill

Now as I was young and easy under the apple boughs
About the lilting house and happy as the grass was green,
 The night above the dingle starry,
  Time let me hail and climb
 Golden in the heydays of his eyes,
And honoured among wagons I was prince of the apple towns
And once below a time I lordly had the trees and leaves
  Trail with daisies and barley
 Down the rivers of the windfall light.

And as I was green and carefree, famous among the barns
About the happy yard and singing as the farm was home,
 In the sun that is young once only,
  Time let me play and be
 Golden in the mercy of his means,
And green and golden I was huntsman and herdsman, the calves
Sang to my horn, the foxes on the hills barked clear and cold,
  And the sabbath rang slowly
 In the pebbles of the holy streams.

All the sun long it was running, it was lovely, the hay
Fields high as the house, the tunes from the chimneys, it was air
 And playing, lovely and watery
  And fire green as grass.
 And nightly under the simple stars
As I rode to sleep the owls were bearing the farm away,
All the moon long I heard, blessed among stables, the nightjars
 Flying with the ricks, and the horses
  Flashing into the dark.

And then to awake, and the farm, like a wanderer white
With the dew, come back, the cock on his shoulder: it was all
   Shining, it was Adam and maiden,
     The sky gathered again
   And the sun grew round that very day.
So it must have been after the birth of the simple light
In the first, spinning place, the spellbound horses walking warm
   Out of the whinnying green stable
     On to the fields of praise.

And honoured among foxes and pheasants by the gay house
Under the new made clouds and happy as the heart was long,
   In the sun born over and over,
     I ran my heedless ways,
   My wishes raced through the house high hay
And nothing I cared, at my sky blue trades, that time allows
In all his tuneful turning so few and such morning songs
   Before the children green and golden
     Follow him out of grace,

Nothing I cared, in the lamb white days, that time would take me
Up to the swallow thronged loft by the shadow of my hand,
   In the moon that is always rising,
     Nor that riding to sleep
   I should hear him fly with the high fields
And wake to the farm forever fled from the childless land.
Oh as I was young and easy in the mercy of his means,
    Time held me green and dying
   Though I sang in my chains like the sea.

Dylan Thomas

Acquainted with the Night *by* Robert Frost

The poem that's been a friend to Glyn Maxwell

Frost is hugely important and influential to me. He captivated me because his poems are so physical. You can sense somebody walking across a field; you can feel the air, the weather and the light.

When I discovered Frost, I immersed myself in his work. I got one of those old Caedmon vinyl records that they made in the fifties and sixties, and it was all in Frost's voice. It's a very ringing and resonant voice. So I knew the poems by heart at the time, just by listening over and over.

'Acquainted with the Night' is about the most formal Frost poem there is. Form is corporeal, bodily; it's an expression of the creature, whether it's the footsteps of metre, or the pulse, or the breaths of the lines. Not only is this a sonnet but it's also in terza rima, an incredibly woven form. It's a great walking metre and of course, this is a walking poem. You can hear him walking through the night in a small American town with no one around. It's metrically regular; it has simple rhymes and vocabulary. At the same time, it feels psychologically acute, and true. Nothing is being compromised to make the form work.

The speaker is troubled by something that he never explains to us or to the watchman. It's not exactly a cry for help. It is a cry, but one he never explains. He simply gives you the experience of it – 'Yes, I've been acquainted with the night and life is terrifying.'

It's a kind of perfection to me, this poem. When you find a poem you love, it really is like an encounter with someone that sticks with you, and you think, 'Oh, I want to see that person again.'

Acquainted with the Night

I have been one acquainted with the night.
I have walked out in rain—and back in rain.
I have outwalked the furthest city light.

I have looked down the saddest city lane.
I have passed by the watchman on his beat
And dropped my eyes, unwilling to explain.

I have stood still and stopped the sound of feet
When far away an interrupted cry
Came over houses from another street,

But not to call me back or say good-bye;
And further still at an unearthly height,
One luminary clock against the sky

Proclaimed the time was neither wrong nor right.
I have been one acquainted with the night.

Robert Frost

Mushrooms *by* Sylvia Plath

The poem that's been a friend to Jenny Woods

I keep coming back to Sylvia Plath and I never lose that first response I had as a teenager, the excitement of discovering how amazing language can be. We know a lot about her tragic history, but I think she had this wonderful playfulness and there's such joy in her use of language that I've always found exhilarating.

Through the rhythm and imagery in 'Mushrooms' she's captured this quiet but pressured resistance and growth. This sense of the wonder and power of people and things that are quiet, meek, under the surface. These hidden lives that are actually part of a collective movement that pushes.

It's the duality of that light, softness – 'Whitely, discreetly, / Very quietly' – that is also pushing, and pushing you on in the poem. It keeps moving forward and as you read it, you feel this quiet surge upwards. It's the masses underneath the surface, these interior lives that are all connected, all nudging and shoving and multiplying. I think that's something that you want to hear now – a sense of hope almost, but not a sentimental one. It's more real, earthy. It's the kind of poetry that stirs something in you. There will always be obstacles and you might even be your own obstacle, but there's a way through.

There's nothing glamorous here. There's a sense of domesticity, of workmanship. The mushrooms are shelves and tables and they're not beautiful things, there's no flourish, but there's something pleasurable in that these are the ones that inherit the earth. There is tremendous power in that repetition of 'So many of us! So many of us!' It's like she's saying, hear it again! I love that.

It's my very small little friend who's always there, smoothing the covers, tucking me in and holding my hand.

Mushrooms

Overnight, very
Whitely, discreetly,
Very quietly

Our toes, our noses
Take hold on the loam,
Acquire the air.

Nobody sees us,
Stops us, betrays us;
The small grains make room.

Soft fists insist on
Heaving the needles,
The leafy bedding,

Even the paving.
Our hammers, our rams,
Earless and eyeless,

Perfectly voiceless,
Widen the crannies,
Shoulder through holes. We

Diet on water,
On crumbs of shadow,
Bland-mannered, asking

Little or nothing.
So many of us!
So many of us!

We are shelves, we are
Tables, we are meek,
We are edible,

Nudgers and shovers
In spite of ourselves.
Our kind multiplies:

We shall by morning
Inherit the earth.
Our foot's in the door.

Sylvia Plath

Acknowledgements

There have been many exceptional and generous people who have been part of the last ten years of The Poetry Exchange and without whom this book would not exist.

We have been blessed to work with our wonderful producer, John Prebble. His sensitivity, attention to detail and belief in the power of poetry to bring people closer to themselves, and to one another, has been a guiding force for this project and this book. We are indebted to him, and also to the creative talent and energy of Sally Anglesea who was with the project from the start. Our warm thanks to Beth Cuenco, founder of Wise Words festival, where the idea of poems as friends was born. Thanks too to Bridget Floyer and Jessica Boatright, both of whom have supported the project with rigour and imagination.

Our podcast editor Ben Hales has been a constant listening presence, and without his deft and skilful work we would not have been able to grow such a far-reaching audience. Our heartfelt thanks to that community of listeners who have shared the podcast and written notes of encouragement letting us know that what we do is making a difference.

The Poetry Exchange became a charitable project in 2019, and since then we have been honoured to have the guidance and expertise of our three brilliant trustees: Roy McFarlane, Alison McManus and Andrea Witzke Slot.

We are surrounded by a tremendous array of talent in the poets, actors and artists who have been part of our wider team. Alongside our trustees, they include: Victoria Field, Degna Stone, Martin Heaney, Sarah Salway, Alastair Snell, Hafsah Aneela Bashir, Sarah Butler, Natasha Gordon, Luke Pell, Jacqueline Kington, Rebecca Manley, Subhadassi, Alex McIntyre and Katherine Goda.

We are grateful to Arts Council England for the part it has played in funding the development of The Poetry Exchange and to Jan Kofi-Tsekpo for her tremendous support. Our thanks also to all the partners who have hosted events and conversations, online and in person, including: Manchester Central Library, Latitude Festival, the National Poetry Library, the Birmingham and Midland Institute, the National Centre for Writing and Durham Book Festival.

There is a number of very special friends to the project whose ambassadorial skills, vision and generosity have helped to grow the work in ways we could not have imagined or managed without. They include: Cas Donald, Shaun Flint, Diana Bennett, Julie Smith, Sue Lawther-Brown, Maria Augusta Arruda and Charlie Beaumont.

Support and friendship to the project has also generously been given by: William Tuckett, Karen da Silva, Jo Bell, Malika Booker, Tamar Yoseloff, Sasha Dugdale, Ciarán Hinds, Karen McCarthy Woolf, Tobias Menzies, John McAuliffe, Ella Donald, Peggy Hughes, Tim Baker and the members of our Muse Club.

The lifeblood of The Poetry Exchange is the conversations we have and the nominations we receive. Inevitably it has not been possible to include all of these in this volume, but we are no less grateful to those people for enriching our work.

Our thanks to Zoë Blanc, Nina Sandelson and Ana Sampson at Quercus for embracing the intricacies and vision of this anthology with rigour and sensitivity.

Thanks also to the brilliant Ken Cockburn, who has brought grace, patience and resilience to the detailed task of securing permissions to feature the poems.

Our thanks again to our contributors here who have shared their connection to their chosen poem, and to the brilliant poets, publishers and estates who have allowed us to feature their work.

And last but not least, thank you to you, our readers and our listeners, for making all this possible and for bringing us the gift of companionship with poems as friends.

Permission Credits

The editors and publisher gratefully acknowledge the following for permission to reprint copyright material:

Adrienne Rich: *What is Found There; Notebooks on Poetry and Politics*, W.W. Norton and Company, Inc. 2003. Used by permission of W. W. Norton & Company, Inc. **Kim Addonizio:** 'You Don't Know What Love Is' from *What Is This Thing Called Love: Poems*. Copyright © 2014 by Kim Addonizio. Used by permission of W. W. Norton & Company, Inc. **Elizabeth Alexander:** 'Ars Poetica #100: I Believe' © 2005 by Elizabeth Alexander, is used with the permission of the Author, and was first published in 2005 in *American Sublime* by Elizabeth Alexander and subsequently published by Graywolf Press in *Crave Radiance, New and Selected Poems 1990–2010*, © Elizabeth Alexander. **Nazik al-Mala'ika:** 'Love Song for Words', translated by Rebecca C. Johnson, from *Checkpoints: Literature from Iraq*, Words Without Borders, 2003. Copyright © 2003 by Nazik al-Mala'ika. Translation copyright © 2003 by Rebecca C. Johnson. **Jean 'Binta' Breeze:** 'Truth' from *Third World Girl: Selected Poems*, Bloodaxe Books, 2011. Reproduced by permission of Bloodaxe Books. www.bloodaxebooks.com. **Hera Lindsay Bird:** 'Pyramid Scheme' from *Pamper Me to Hell & Back*, Smith/Doorstop Books, 2018. **Gwendolyn Brooks:** 'Old Mary'. Reprinted by consent of Brooks Permissions. **Martin Carter:** 'Proem' from *University of Hunger: Collected Poems & Selected Prose*, edited by Gemma Robinson, Bloodaxe Books, 2006. Reproduced by permission of Bloodaxe Books. www.bloodaxebooks. com. **C. P. Cavafy:** 'Return', translated by Rae Dalven, from *The Complete Poems of Cavafy*. Copyright © 1948, 1949, 1959, 1961 by Rae Dalven. Used by permission of HarperCollins Publishers. **Linda Chase:** 'The Young Taoist Transcends His Body' from *Extended Family*, Carcanet Press, 2011. **Carol Ann Duffy:** 'Prayer' from *Collected Poems*, Picador, 2015. Copyright © Carol Ann Duffy. Reproduced by permission of the author c/o Rogers, Coleridge & White Ltd., 20 Powis Mews, London WII IJN. **Roxy Dunn:** '5AM' from *Clowning*, Eyewear Publishing, 2016. Reproduced by kind permission of the author. **Paul Durcan:** 'The Death by Heroin of Sid Vicious' from *A Snail in my Prime: New and Selected Poems*, Harvill Press, 2011. **T. S. Eliot:** 'The Love Song of J. Alfred Prufrock' from *Collected Poems 1909–1962*, Faber & Faber, 2002. **Robert Frost:** 'Acquainted with the Night' from *The Poetry of Robert Frost*, edited by Edward Connery Lathem. Copyright © 1928, 1969 by Henry

Index of Poets

Index of Contributors